BIBLE KEY WORDS

IX. SPIRIT OF GOD

BIBLE KEY WORDS
FROM GERHARD KITTEL'S
*THEOLOGISCHES WÖRTERBUCH
ZUM NEUEN TESTAMENT*

SPIRIT OF GOD

BY

EDUARD SCHWEIZER

AND OTHERS

ADAM & CHARLES BLACK
LONDON

FIRST PUBLISHED 1960
A. AND C. BLACK LIMITED
4, 5 AND 6 SOHO SQUARE, LONDON W.1

Translation from the German
by A. E. Harvey

PRINTED IN GREAT BRITAIN BY
WILLIAM CLOWES AND SONS, LIMITED, LONDON AND BECCLES

TRANSLATOR'S PREFACE

THE article on πνεῦμα is one of the longest in Kittel's *Wörterbuch*, and in order to bring it within the range of this series, it has been necessary to omit some of the material. The principle I have followed is to include only those parts which are directly relevant to the concept of the Spirit of God (hence the title of this book). Thus, the long contribution by Hermann Kleinknecht on the word πνεῦμα in Greek literature, and also that by Werner Bieder on πνεῦμα in the Septuagint and Hellenistic Judaism, have been omitted altogether, since they throw light more on the history of the word than on the development of the concept. This translation therefore begins with the section by Friedrich Baumgärtel on the Old Testament (omitting only the purely lexicographical material); this is followed by a part of Erik Sjöberg's section on Rabbinic Judaism; and the remainder represents the important contribution of Eduard Schweizer, culminating in his exhaustive treatment of πνεῦμα in the New Testament. Here, the only omissions are a few notes and references to the work of German scholars. I hope that this principle of selection will not have frustrated the intention of the authors; its justification is that it makes it possible to present to the English reader their important and stimulating discussion of the Spirit of God.

The compression and exhaustiveness required by the *Wörterbuch* make the original German not always easy to read. I have done my best to make this translation as lucid as possible for the reader. Detailed discussions of particular passages are printed (as in the German) in smaller type, and may be passed over at a first reading.

Untranslated quotations in Greek and Hebrew are avoided in the main text, and (on the assumption that readers of German will not be using this book anyway) all references to untranslated German works have been omitted, except for a few standard commentaries and works of reference. Even so, I am aware that much of the book is far from easy reading; but further simplification would have distorted the original, and I can only hope that the reader will persevere through all complexities of the subject and inelegancies of translation, and will gain for himself, as I have, a richer understanding of the Holy Spirit.

A. E. HARVEY

CONTENTS

vii

BIBLIOGRAPHY

GENERAL

E. DE W. BURTON, *Spirit, Soul and Flesh. . . in Greek writings and translated works from the earliest period to 180 A.D.* (1918).

LINDSAY DEWAR, *The Holy Spirit and Modern Thought* (1959).

C. H. DODD, *The Interpretation of the Fourth Gospel* (1953), 213–27.

H. B. SWETE, Article, *Holy Spirit*, in Hastings' *Dictionary of the Bible*.

OLD TESTAMENT

N. H. SNAITH, *The Distinctive Ideas of the Old Testament* (1944), ch. vii.

J. PEDERSEN, *Israel* I/II (1926), 102–106.

TH. C. VRIEZEN, *Outline of O. T. Theology*, E.T. 249–51.

JUDAISM ETC.

J. ABELSON, *The Immanence of God in Rabbinical Literature* (1912), 174–277.

L. BLAU, Article, *Holy Spirit*, in the *Jewish Encyclopaedia*, VI 447–50.

W. D. DAVIES, *Paul and the Dead Sea Scrolls: Flesh and Spirit*, in *The Scrolls and the New Testament*, ed. K. Stendahl (1958), 171–82.

G. F. MOORE, *Judaism* (1927 ff.), I 237, 247, 371–2, 401–13, 421–2, 445–59, 485–9; II 287–322, 353, 384, 389–90.   (cited: Moore).

G. F. MOORE, *Intermediaries in Jewish Theology*, H.Th.R. 15 (1922), 41–85.

NEW TESTAMENT

C. K. BARRETT, *The Holy Spirit and the Gospel Tradition* (1947) (cited: *Gospel Tradition*).

C. K. BARRETT, *The Holy Spirit in the Fourth Gospel*, J.T.S. N.S. 1 (1950) 1–15.

E. W. BULLINGER, *The Spirit and his Gifts* (1953).

R. BULTMANN, *Theology of the New Testament*, E.T. I 153–64, 203–10, 333–9 (cited: *T.N.T.*).

E. DE W. BURTON, *Commentary on Galatians* (I.C.C.) 486–92.

H. E. DANA, *The Holy Spirit in Acts* (1943).

J. E. FISON, *The Blessing of the Holy Spirit* (1950).

F. J. FOAKES-JACKSON and K. LAKE, *The Beginnings of Christianity* (1920–1923) (cited: Jackson-Lake).

W. F. HOWARD, *Christianity according to St. John* (1943).

G. W. H. LAMPE, *The Seal of the Spirit* (1951).

G. W. H. LAMPE, *The Holy Spirit in the Writings of St. Luke*, in: *Studies in the Gospels*, ed. D. E. Nineham (1955).

E. SCHWEIZER, *The Spirit of Power*, Interpretation 6 (1952) 259–78.

E. F. SCOTT, *The Spirit in the New Testament* (1923).

H. B. SWETE, *The Holy Spirit in the New Testament* (1909).

ABBREVIATIONS

Bl.-Debr.	F. Blass, *Grammatik des Neutestamentlichen Griechisch*, bearbeitet von A. Debrunner
Bousset-Gressmann	W. Bousset, *Die Religion des Judentums im späthellenistischen Zeitalter*, herausgegeben von H. Gressmann (1926)
C.H.	Corpus Hermeticum
Exp.	The Expositor
Exp.T.	The Expository Times
H.Th.R.	The Harvard Theological Review
I.C.C.	International Critical Commentary
J.B.L.	Journal of Biblical Literature
J.Q.R.	Jewish Quarterly Review
J.T.S.	Journal of Theological Studies (N.S.: New Series)
N.T.St.	New Testament Studies
Rev. Bib.	Revue Biblique
R.H.Ph.R.	Revue d'Histoire et de Philosophie religieuses
R.H.R.	Revue de l'Histoire des Religions
Str.-B.	H. L. Strack and P. Billerbeck, *Kommentar zum N.T. aus Talmud und Midrasch*.
Z.N.W.	Zeitschrift für Neutestamentliche Wissenschaft
LXX	Septuagint
E.T.	English Translation
[ ]	enclose additional notes by the Translator

THE OLD TESTAMENT

"THE Egyptians are men (אדם) and not God (אל), and their horses are flesh (בשר) and not spirit (רוח)" says Isaiah (xxxi. 3). "Flesh" is earthly fragility and weakness —its bearer is "man"; "spirit" is absolute power and majesty—its bearer is "God". Thus gains expression the dynamic element which is contained in the Spirit of God (רוח יהוה), and which is perceptible in the working of this Spirit: the Spirit of God turns the desert into a paradise, and makes it an abode of justice and righteousness (Isa. xxxii. 15 ff.).

But the concept is not only dynamic, it is also ethical (cf. Isa. xxx. 1: where plans are carried out, which are not of the Spirit of God, there sin is heaped up). The Spirit of God is a creative, transforming power (cf. Ps. li. 12–13), and its purpose is to create a sphere of religion and morals. In this sense, the Spirit of God rests upon the Messiah as the "spirit of counsel and might" and as the "spirit of knowledge and the fear of the Lord" (Isa. xi. 2); and in this sense it is at work through the Servant of God (Isa. xlii. 1 ff.). Israel's destiny is fulfilled through the Spirit of God, which transforms hearts of stone into hearts of flesh, and changes the nation into a community devoted to God (Ezek. xxxvi. 26–7).[1]

Yet it would not be true to say that according to the prophets the Spirit of God will only give free rein to its life-giving power in the New Age. The transformation of the nation into a true People of God comes to pass the moment the nation is judged; and the prophets see this

---

[1] Cf. also Isa. iv. 2 ff.; xliv. 3; Zech. xii. 10.

judgment as something already being carried out—the present already anticipates the future. Isa. xxxi. 3— and similarly xxx. 1 ff.—implies both promise and judgment at the same time: for the prophets, each is equally a present manifestation of the operation of the Spirit of God.

Up to this point the principle is clear, especially in the major prophets: the Spirit of God is power, power with a moral emphasis. It is active power, that is to say, it is the personal activity of God's will, achieving a moral and religious object. It impinges on Israel as the power of history; for the transformation to the new state of affairs, the creation of the "New Spirit",[1] takes place by means of the judgment of God fulfilled in historical events; and this transformation means the end, and at the same time the consummation, of the history of Israel. Thus any polytheistic sense of a divine power immanent in the world is ruled out; and the acknowledgment of any such power is regarded as an escape from the active, personal power of God's will, from his absolute *majestas*, and therefore as a rebellion of the will against God, as sin. At the same time, the idea that divine powers can be regularly present in man is also ruled out. This is the opposite of Egyptian and Babylonian religion, where the king is the incarnation of divine power. In Israel there is no God-man. Man is subject to this power, but he is not identified with it, he is "flesh" and not "spirit". Moreover, the Spirit of God, as the operation of God's will, may be perceptible, but it is inscrutable. You cannot say when it operates or how it operates. Both the terminology and the content of the prophetic message are always indefinite; its diversity, even inconsistency, cannot be removed by any attempt at harmonization. The dynamic element of the Spirit of God is or will be perceptible, but its logic is a mystery. It is the untrammelled, incalculable operation of God's will. The when and the how of God's "plan" remains a

[1] Ezek. xi. 19; xviii. 31; xxxvi. 26; Ps. li. 12.

secret; but the reality of his activity and power is indisputable.

The second characteristic of the Spirit of God is brought out by the priestly writer in the sentence, "The Spirit of God moved over the water" (Gen. i. 2). Here, as before, the Spirit of God is grasped as a dynamic and creative principle. But it is not a matter only, or even principally, of the activity of God's will completing the creation of the universe (cf. Ps. xxxiii. 6); it is much more the fact that this dynamic force is responsible for all that is alive, for all physical life. The Spirit of God is the active principle which proceeds from God and gives life to the physical world (Gen. ii. 7[1]). It is implicitly connected with the phrase, "and God spake", דבר יהוה. God creates "by the breath of his mouth" (ברוח פיו Ps. xxxiii. 6, parallel to "by the word of God", בדבר יהוה). But by the activity of his Spirit, God also sustains his creation: if God should take back his Spirit (רוח), his breath (נשמה), to himself, all flesh would perish (Job xxxiv. 14; cf. Ps. civ. 29–30). "The Spirit of God has created me, and the breath of the Almighty gives me life" (Job xxxiii. 4).

In this connection the same definition holds good, of the Spirit of God as the creative, active, personal power of God. This excludes any belief in divine powers, in the sense of an understanding of the universe and the natural order based on pantheism, myth and mysticism. No immanent, divine forces of nature exist. By contrast with the neighbouring religions, nature has no power in it, no God in it.

Here, too, God's creative power is a free gift. But here, too, it is inscrutable, even uncanny. There are limits to the gift of the Spirit (Gen. vi. 3). There is no way of discovering when God may take back his "breath". The divine activity is discoverable and perceptible, but inscrutable.

All this is fundamental.

[1] Compare Gen. ii. 7 נשמת חיים with Gen. vi. 17 רוח חיים.

However, there is an example of Israel experiencing the activity of the Spirit of God in history in another way, and this time we miss the previous emphasis on an ethical and religious factor.[1] At a time when there is still no territorial kingdom, God raises up charismatic leaders for the people, and enables them, with his Spirit, to act for a national or political cause. Othniel (Judges iii. 10), Gideon (vi. 34), Jephtha (xi. 29) and Saul (I Sam. xi. 6) are examples. David, too, has the Spirit of God come upon him when he is anointed by Samuel (I Sam. xvi. 13). Here again, the Spirit is logically inscrutable, incalculable; it gives a share of itself as and to whom it will. Men who up to now have been completely unnoticed suddenly come forward as leaders under the working of the Spirit.

The sudden and uncanny side of the Spirit's activity receives special emphasis in the description of ecstatic experiences. The subject of an ecstatic experience is called "a man of the Spirit" (איש הרוח Hos. ix. 7). The Spirit of God comes mightily on Saul (צלח על), so that he falls into ecstasy (I Sam. x. 6, 10). Samson's giant strength breaks forth suddenly in ecstatic excitement, and is the effect of the Spirit of God (Judges xiv. 6, 19; xv. 14 —where the expression is again צלח על). A theoretical analysis of the working of the Spirit may be found in Num. xi. 24 ff. (E): God takes some of the Spirit which is in Moses, and apportions it to the seventy elders, who fall into an ecstasy. The ecstasy then spreads infectiously. The reference is also to ecstatic experience in those passages in which the Spirit of God causes prophetic utterance,[2] or snatches a man away (Ezek. iii. 14). Here again the Spirit of God is manifested as the unpredictable and irresistible working of God's power, often even with a touch of the demonic about it. The activity of the Spirit

---

[1] Nevertheless this factor is still present in Israel's national consciousness; for the "Holy War" is an institution with its roots in cult. Cf. G. v. Rad, *Der Heilige Krieg im alten Israel* (1951), 29–33.

[2] Gen. xli. 38; II Sam. xxiii. 2; I Kings xxii. 24; Num. xxiv. 2; Isa. lxi. 1; Ezek. xi. 5; Joel iii. 1–2; II Chron. xxiv. 20.

of God can be easily traced and perceived, but the logic
of why, when and for how long it comes, is inscrutable.

These last observations bring us into the sphere of the
phenomena of comparative religion; for the neighbouring
religions are also aware of the operation of God's power.
Ecstatic experience can hardly have had its origin in
Israel, or even in the other Semitic religions: Indo-
Germanic religions present a much more likely field.

It is not by chance that Hebrew expresses "spirit" and
"wind" by the same concept רוח. The wind is powerful,
with a power that cannot be withstood; moreover it is
mysterious: "the wind blows where it wills, and you hear
the sound of it, but you do not know whence it comes or
whither it goes" (John iii. 8). To this extent, any
mysterious, unpredictable power is one with the wind.
The divine stirrings are a *breathing* (רוח) of God, and they
are recognized in neighbouring religions as divine powers
and forces that bring salvation or destruction.   Israel with
its spirit-faith has its roots deep in its surroundings.

The major prophets took the spirit-concept out of these
surroundings, and transformed the divine spirit from something religiously and ethically neutral into the concept of
the purposeful and deliberate operation of God's personal
power.   The Spirit of God is the concept (however much
it resists logical analysis) for the activity of the one and
only God in history and creation.   In fact, it can serve as
a direct expression for God's inner being and for his present
reality.[1]

"Is God's Spirit too short?" (הקצר רוח יהוה, Mic. ii. 7)
was once the threat uttered against Micah by his opponents.   Now that judgment had been passed on the
people, faith held fast to the belief that the Spirit of God
is not "too short", that (despite all appearances) God
in his Spirit is present as Lord of history.   God keeps to
his promise, the promise out of which his Spirit has

---

[1] Cf. Ps. cxxxix. 7, where רוח יהוה is used in parallel to פני יהוה.

fashioned history and will lead it to its destined end. The Spirit of God, as God's mighty and irresistible saving activity, becomes a source of help and strength: "My Spirit is in the midst of you, be not afraid!" (Hag. ii. 5), "Not by might nor by power, but by my Spirit shall it happen" (Zech. iv. 6), the Spirit of God gathers all God's people together (Zech. vi. 1 ff.). The Spirit of God is the seal of God's faithfulness to his covenant (Isa. lix. 21).

One further strand remains to be indicated in the concept of the Spirit of God in Israel. If the Old Testament has taken the power out of all cosmic and earthly dominions and powers, it has anchored the demonic firmly in the Almighty power, that is to say, in the Spirit of God. The Spirit of God can become active as an Evil Spirit (רוח רעה Judges ix. 23; I Sam. xvi. 14 ff.; xviii. 10). This Evil Spirit is found eventually opposed to God and is hypostatized: in I Kings xxii. 19 ff. "the Spirit" comes forward from the host standing around God and offers himself to be a lying spirit in the mouth of the prophets. In an exactly similar situation, the book of Job (i. 6 ff.) uses the concept "Satan" for the incarnation of this Evil Spirit of God.[1]

[1] "Satan" becomes the heading under which this strand of Israel's spirit-theology must be followed up. See the article διάβολος in Kittel.

BETWEEN THE OLD AND NEW TESTAMENTS[1]

THE Jews were confronted inescapably by the Old Testament message that God and his Spirit are extraneous to man. Being seized of God is an effect of grace, not of nature. So much was implied in the proposition that the soul of man proceeds from the Spirit of God. But at this point a problem arose which was to be a source of trouble for generations. As soon as the soul became, no longer just the life-force, but the personally responsible Self which even survives death, the following questions became burning issues: if the soul is a part of God's Spirit, must it not be saved automatically? Or is there another human self to be distinguished from it, which can either absorb or expel, either keep pure or defile, this part of the Spirit of God? Or must this part of the Spirit of God be understood as the possibility of free decision? How can the actual working of the Spirit of God be distinguished from this? How is life after death to be conceived of?

These questions are wrestled with in Judaism, in Gnosticism and in the New Testament.

A. RABBINIC JUDAISM

In Rabbinic thought, "the Spirit" is essentially the prophetic Spirit which speaks in the Old Testament.[2] All the writings in the Old Testament are inspired by the Spirit,[3] and the question whether a particular writing

---

[1] This heading is convenient, if inexact: many of the writings referred to are later than the N.T., but are nevertheless valuable for elucidating pre-N.T. ideas.

[2] Gen. xli. 38; II Sam. xxiii. 2; I Kings xxii. 24 (cf. II Chron. xviii. 23); Num. xxiv. 2; Isa. lxi. 1; Ezek. xi. 5; Joel iii. 1–2; II Chron. xxiv. 20.

[3] Cant. R. i. 1, §5–10; Lev. R. xv. 2 on xiii. 2 (Str.-B. II, 134 f.; IV, 444). Cf. IV Ezra xiv. 21; Apoc. Jos. i. 41.

should be taken into the Canon is identical with the
question whether it was written in the Holy Spirit.[1] Consequently, a saying from the Old Testament can be quoted
either as a saying of the Torah or as a saying of the Holy
Spirit.[2] However, the fact that the Holy Scriptures as a
whole are inspired by the Holy Spirit does not prevent
certain passages being read as the utterances of different
speakers, of whom the Holy Spirit may be one. One
sentence in the text may be understood as a statement
made by Israel (or other persons or groups), and another
as a reply made by the Holy Spirit. For example, in
Deut. xxi, verse 7 is taken as spoken by the elders in the
city concerned, 8α by the priests and 8β by the Holy
Spirit. In Judges v, verse 28β is spoken by Sisera's
mother, 29 by his wife and daughter, and 31α by the
Holy Spirit.[3] It is also possible to put two different texts
together, taking one as a statement by Israel, the other as
the subsequent reply of the Holy Spirit. In this case the
texts concerned are ones which exalt God on the one hand
and Israel on the other. For instance, in Deut. vi. 4
("Hear, O Israel . . . .") Israel confesses Yahweh to be
the one true God; the answer of the Holy Spirit is in II
Sam. vii. 3, where it calls Israel a people unique on earth.[4]
In statements like these, the Holy Spirit is God's represen-
tative and expresses his reaction to what has been said and
done, though without being identified with him.[5]

Another factor in Rabbinic thought is the relation between the Holy Spirit and a God-fearing life. From this

[1] T. Yad. ii. 14 (Str.-B. II, 135); B. Meg. 7a.
[2] It must not be concluded from this that the Torah was identified with
the Holy Spirit, as J. Abelson does (*The Immanence of God in Rabbinical
Literature*, 225).
[3] T. Sota, ix. 2–3, 9; J. Sota, ix. 7 (23d/24a). See H. Parzen, J.Q.R.
20 (1929/30), 56–60.
[4] M. Ex. xv. 2 (ed. Horowitz and Rabin (1931), 126); Sifre Deut. 335
on xxxiii. 26 (ed. M. Friedmann (1864), 148a). Cf. Str.-B. II, 136.
[5] Nevertheless it is also possible for a passage of Scripture to be interpreted in such a way that certain words in it are spoken by the Holy Spirit
to God himself. Examples of this appear in the very few passages in
Rabbinic Literature where the Spirit appears as an Advocate before God:
Lev. R. vi. 1 on v. i; Deut. R. iii. 11 on ix. 1.

angle, the gift of the Spirit is thought of principally as a reward for a life of obedience. In the first instance, the possession of the Spirit is represented as a consequence of a just life, not as a cause of it; but naturally, once it is given to a man, it inspires him still more to holiness of life. Where the Holy Spirit is, there there are devout and just men; and where there are just men, there the Holy Spirit is bestowed. At the edge of the Red Sea the Israelites had faith: therefore the Holy Spirit rested upon them. From this R. Nehemiah draws the general conclusion: "Whoever submits to a command in faith is worthy that the Holy Spirit should rest upon him."[1] "Whoever studies [the Torah] with intent to perform it earns the gift of the Holy Spirit", says R. Aha.[2] "Whoever sacrifices himself for Israel will receive the reward of honour, greatness and the Holy Spirit."[3]

When the devout man sins, the Holy Spirit departs from him[4]; the same happens when he approaches a place which is under the power of sin.[5] The Spirit cannot be effectual in unclean surroundings; and so (according to a widespread opinion) it is restricted to the land of Israel: outside Palestine there is no divine inspiration.[6] It is true that in the beginning the heathen could also receive the Holy Spirit, and therefore prophets rose up among them.[7] But after Balaam had misused his prophetic gift,

[1] M. Ex. xv. 1 (Horovitz, 114). Cf. Str.–B. II, 135.

[2] Lev. R. xxxv. vii. on xxvi. 3 (Str.–B. II, 134).

[3] Num. R. xv. 20 on xi. 16 (Str.–B. II, 133 f.). Compare with all this the celebrated sequence of R. Phineas b. Jair: "Zeal (in obedience to the Law) leads to bodily purity, which leads to ritual purity, which leads to temperance, which leads to holiness, which leads to humility, which leads to penitence, which leads to piety, which leads to the Holy Spirit, which leads to the Resurrection, which comes by means of the prophet Elijah, of blessed memory." Str.–B. I, 194. Cf. A. Büchler, *Types of Jewish Palestinian Piety*, 42–67.

[4] Gen. R. lx. 3 on xxii. 14 (ed. J. Theodor (1903), 644).

[5] E.g. from Esther, as she approached the palace of the heathen king, Yalḳuṭ Shim'oni, Esth. v. 2, cf. Abelson, *op. cit.* 270. Cf. also Gen. R. lxv on xxvi. 34 (Theodor, 715); R. Joshua b. Levi: the Holy Ghost departed from Isaac on account of Esau.

[6] M. Ex. xii. 1 (Horovitz, 3). Cf. Str.–B. I, 643; Parzen, *op. cit.* 53.

[7] Str.–B. II, 130.

the Holy Spirit was taken away from the heathen and reserved for Israel.[1]

Apart from this, strength and health in body and soul are necessary conditions for possessing the Spirit. "The Holy Spirit rests only on a joyful heart."[2] When Jacob, on the news of Joseph's death, gave himself up to his grief, the Holy Spirit left him.[3] To receive the Holy Spirit you must rejoice at God's command[4]—and with that we are back in the world of ethical religion.

Who then was regarded as having the gift of the Spirit? The answer may be given under three heads: the past, the future and the present.

(a) *The past:* In Jewish thought, the great figures of the Old Testament period were regarded as inspired by the Holy Spirit. Naturally this goes mainly for the prophets (Ecclus. xlviii. 12, 24), but there are also other Old Testament figures who speak under prophetic inspiration. Rebecca blessed Jacob "after the Spirit of truth had entered into her mouth" (Jub. xxv. 14). Isaac blessed Levi and Judah by the Spirit of divination (Jub. xxxi. 12). Joseph had the Spirit of God in him in the form of power to live a moral life: "merciful and compassionate, he never bore a grudge" (Test. Sim. iv. 4). The Rabbis took this conception of the patriarchs a stage further. In their view, all those in the Old Testament who feared God, spoke and acted under the influence of the Holy Spirit. All the devout and the righteous of earlier generations were initiated into the secrets of God through their prophetic gifts.[5] Naturally the great figures in the history

---

[1] Tanḥ. בלק 231a; Num. R. xx. 1 on xxii. 2 (Str.-B. II, 130). According to other authorities this happened after Israel had received the Torah (Str.-B. II, 130) or after the completion of the Tent of Meeting (Cant. R. ii. 3, R. Isaac).

[2] J. Sukka, v. 1 (55a, 63), cf. Str.-B. I, 643.

[3] Gen. R. xli. 6 on xlii. 1 (Theodor, 1121); Tg. J.1. Gen. xlv. 27. Similarly in his last days Jacob forfeited his prophetic gift owing to his age and physical weakness, Gen. R. xcvii on xlviii. 10 (Theodor, 1243).

[4] B. Pes. 117a (Str.-B. III, 312).

[5] Gen. R. xlvii on xlix. 27 (Theodor, 1224); Tanḥ. ויחי 58a (ed. S. Buber (1885), §13, 110a); cf. Str.-B. II, 131–2.

of salvation possessed the Spirit to an exceptional degree. Moses was a prophet, as the Old Testament proved. David and Solomon, as authors of Old Testament scriptures, must have possessed the Holy Spirit.[1]   Only if he possessed the Spirit could a priest successfully give oracles by Urim and Thummim.[2]   The patriarchs possessed it as a matter of course; but their wives also were subject to visions and utterances due to the Holy Spirit.[3]

(b) *The future*: It follows from Isa. xi. 2 that in the Last Age the Messiah will possess the Spirit of God.   This continues to be the Jewish conception, and is documented as much by the apocrypha and pseudepigrapha as by Rabbinic writings.   "The Lord made him mighty in the Holy Spirit", ὁ θεὸς κατειργάσατο αὐτὸν δυνατὸν ἐν πνεύματι ἁγίῳ, says Ps. Sol. xvii. 37 of the Messianic King, cf. Ps. Sol. xviii. 7.   Eth. Enoch xlix. 3 has this expansion of Isa. xi. 2: on the chosen one, the Son of Man, "rests the Spirit of wisdom, and the Spirit which gives insight, and the Spirit of counsel and power, and the Spirit of just men departed", and again (lxii. 2) "the Spirit of righteousness is poured out upon him".   The same is said of the Messiah in Test. Levi xviii. 7 and Test. Judah xxiv. 2.   Tg. Isa. xlii. 1–4 interprets the Servant (עבד) as the Messiah and makes God say of him: "I will make my Holy Spirit rest upon him" (the same in Tg. Isa. xi. 2).   The Targum reflects the general Rabbinic view which is based on Isa. xi. 2.

On the other hand, the Messiah himself is never identified with the Spirit of God—not even in R. Simeon b. Lakish's commentary on Gen. i. 2 (Gen. R. ii. 4; Theodor,

[1] Str.-B. II, 132.
[2] B. Yoma, 73b; Str.-B. II, 132.
[3] Isaac: Gen. R. lxxv. 8 on xxxii. 4 (Theodor, 886); Jacob: lxxxiv. 19 on xxxvii. 33 (Theodor, 1024) and xcviii. 7 on xlii. 11 (Theodor, 1127); Joseph: xciii. 12 on xlv. 14 (Theodor, 1170); Sarah: xlv. 2 on xvi. 2 (Theodor, 449); Rachel: lxxii. 6 on xxx. 31 (Theodor, 845).   Cf. also B. Meg. 14a for the seven prophetesses in Israel: Sarah, Miriam, Deborah, Hannah, Abigail (cf. Eccl. R. iii. 21), Huldah and Esther.   Both Tamar (Gen. R. lxxxv. 9 on xxxviii. 18, Theodor, 1042) and Rahab (Sifre Deut. xxii on i. 24 Friedmann, 69b) prophesied and had visions in the Spirit.

16–17), where he finds the four heathen kingdoms alluded
to in the words which describe the original chaos, and the
Spirit of the Messiah in the Spirit which moved upon the
waters.   Here it would be as wrong to identify the Messiah
with the Spirit of God as it would be to identify the four
heathen kingdoms with the original chaos.[1]

In the Last Age, too, the ransomed righteous will receive
the Spirit of God.   Moral renewal is expected as the result
of a change in the spirit and heart of man.   Some
authorities (e.g. Jub. i. 23; IV Ezra vi. 26) say that this
will be effected by God himself, others that it will be
through the Spirit poured out upon the righteous.   ''The
Spirit of salvation'', ''the Spirit of grace'', will be given
them by God himself (Test. Jud. xxiv. 3) or by his Messiah
(Test. Levi xviii. 11).   It is true that in the apocrypha
and pseudepigrapha the connection between the final
renewal and the gift of the Spirit is not often found,[2] but
this makes the Rabbinic sources all the clearer.   In them,
the pivotal texts from Scripture dealing with future
expectations are Ezek. xxxvi. 26–7 and xxxvii. 14.   These
are the authority for expecting the resurrection to take
place through the Spirit of God.[3]   Ezek. xxxvi. 26–7 is
also the basis for the hope that in the age to come God will
destroy the evil instinct—he will take away the heart of
stone—and will put his Spirit within the Israelites.[4]   This

---

[1] By his interpretation the Rabbi has no intention of describing the events
which accompanied the creation of the world, but is eliciting, by the usual
Rabbinic technique of exposition, the deeper meaning of the text, which is
to be found behind the literal meaning.   This same passage also contains
the message of the enemies of Israel and of the Messiah who will come to
redeem it when it turns to God (which is the meaning of the ''moving
upon the waters'': for according to Lam. ii. 19 the waters contain an
allusion to repentance).   Cf. Str.-B. II, 350.   Nevertheless, it is wrong to
speak as if the Rabbi were interpreting *allegorically*: the Rabbinic view is
that this is a question of the real meaning of the text, and not of arbitrary
fantasies.

[2] There are no other passages besides those mentioned.   The statement
that God will give ''Spirit and Life'' to the devout (II Macc. vii. 23; xiv.
46; Sib. IV, 46, 189) does not refer to the Spirit of God, but to the newly
bestowed life-force of men.

[3] For the Spirit as the power effecting resurrection see above, p. 19, n. 3.

[4] Pesiḳt. 165a; Tanḥ., קדושים, 170b; שלח לך, 216a (Str.-B. III, 240).

leads on the one hand to the Spirit being understood as giving *moral* inspiration, as a power converting the wills of men. But at the same time there are other texts which place in the foreground the *inspirational* power of the Spirit: in the Last Age, all the Israelites will be prophets. For this, Joel iii. 1–2 is the decisive passage of Scripture.[1]

(*c*) *The present:* In the apocrypha and pseudepigrapha, although it is recognized that the great period of prophetic revelation has passed, it is unhesitatingly regarded as a possibility that even now the Spirit may still be granted to men.[2] On the other hand, the Rabbis state explicitly that after the last prophets (Haggai, Zechariah and Malachi) the Holy Spirit has departed from Israel.[3] They even think it possible that the Spirit has never been present in the Second Temple.[4] There can no longer be any revelation inspired by the Spirit which could be put on a level with the Old Testament.

That this was no mere piece of theological speculation but a factor in practical living can be seen from statements that this or that Rabbi would have been worthy of possessing the Holy Spirit, but did not receive it because the present generation is unworthy of it.[5] R. Akiba laments that the Spirit is no longer given even though things are done which ought properly to lead to the gift of it.[6] In fact, however, the view that the Holy Spirit is no longer to be had was not always consistently maintained by the Rabbis.

---

[1] Str.-B. II, 134, 615–6; IV, 915. The same in Sib. III, 582.

[2] E.g. Wisd. ix. 17; vii. 7; Ecclus. xxxix. 6.

[3] T. Sota, xiii. 2. Cf. Str.-B. I, 127.

[4] B. Joma, xxi. b; J. Taan, ii. 1 (65a, 59). Cf. Str.-B. II, 133. Eccles. R. xii. 7 end: after the destruction of the First Temple the Holy Spirit departed from Israel (Str.-B. II, 133).

[5] This is said of Hillel and of Samuel the Little. T. Sota, xiii. 3–4. Cf. Str.-B. I, 129. According to T. Sota, xiii. 4, Samuel the Little did in fact prophesy in the hour of death, and possess some measure of inspiration by the Holy Spirit (Str.-B. II, 133).

[6] B. Sanh. 65b. The same occurs in Sifre Deut. clxxiii on xviii. 11 (Friedmann, 107b) as a saying of R. Eleazar b. Azariah.

The conception of the Spirit as the agent of the divine creation is to be found in the apocrypha and pseudepigrapha (Judith xvi. 14; Wisdom i. 7; xii. 1; Syr. Baruch xxi. 4), and the belief that the Spirit was instrumental in the Creation must also have been current in Palestinian Judaism, and could be derived from the Old Testament. But there are very few instances of it, and this function of the Spirit definitely recedes in importance compared with the conception of the Spirit as the bearer of prophetic revelation and as an endowment of the devout. In early Rabbinic literature the "cosmic" function of the Spirit does not appear to be mentioned at all.[1]

In Gen. i. 2 רוח is normally understood as "wind".[2] R. Simeon b. Lakish, on the basis of Ps. cxxxix. 5, takes it to mean Adam's Spirit, which was the first of God's creations, while his body (according to Gen. i. 26) was the last.[3] Tg.J. I and II Gen. i. 2 paraphrase "the Spirit of God" by "the Spirit of the mercy of JHWH", and so discern in this passage the thought that God has created the world *with mercy*.[4]

A striking development in Judaism is the way in which the Spirit becomes an independent person. In Rabbinic literature the Spirit is often spoken of in personal categories. There are a mass of instances of the Holy Spirit speaking, crying out, warning, lamenting, weeping, rejoicing, consoling and so on.[5] Indeed the Spirit can even be represented as speaking to God.[6] For this reason it has often been maintained that in Judaism the Spirit is conceived of as a hypostasis, or even as a personal angelic being.[7] But this is to bring in conceptions which are

---

[1] Str.-B. I, 48–9.
[2] Tg. O. Gen. i. 2; Gen. R. i. 9 on i. 1 etc.
[3] Tanḥ. תזריע, 153a (ed. S. Buber, 1885, §2, 16b); Midr. Ps. cxxxix. 5 (ed. S. Buber, 1891, 265a).
[4] Str.-B. I, 48–9. Cf. Moore, *Judaism*, I, 389.
[5] Cf. Abelson, 224–37; Str.-B. II, 134–8.
[6] Lev. R. vi. 1 on v. 1; Deut. R. iii. 11 on ix. 1.
[7] E.g. by Ringren, *Word and Wisdom*, 165; against this, Str.-B. II, 134–5; Moore, I, 415–37; Moore, H. Th. R. 15 (1922), 55; Abelson, *op. cit.* 224–37.

strange to the Jewish way of thinking. The Spirit is no
angelic heavenly being. In Jewish literature it never
appears in the heavenly assembly before the throne of God.
It could perhaps be called a hypostasis, if by that one
means its independent activity; but this again is a concept
taken from an un-Jewish range of ideas, and leads easily
to misconceptions. What is intended by using personal
categories to describe the activity of the Spirit is not to
represent it as a particular heavenly being, but rather as
an objective divine reality which encounters a man and
lays claim to him. Its presence can equally be described
by impersonal expressions: it rests (שרה) on a man, it
fills him (מלא), it illuminates him (גצנץ), it shines
upon a place (הופיע). But this does not mean that any
concept of the Spirit is presupposed other than that which
lies behind the personal expressions. What is of critical
importance is that here a man is confronted by a reality
which comes to him from God; a reality which to some
extent represents the presence of God, and yet is not
identical with him.

B. THE DEAD SEA SCROLLS

Already in the later parts of the Old Testament more
and more importance is being attached to the concept that
the Spirit of Yahweh is not only a supernatural power but
is also an ethical power.[1] The further we penetrate into
late Judaism, the more important becomes the ethical
decision of the individual, his choice between Good and
Evil. During the 200 years that Israel lived under Persian
domination, the Persian conception of two opposed spirits [2]
which impinge on a man and between which he has to
choose must have seemed an ideal expression of this idea.[3]
The Spirit is represented as something continually present,

---

[1] Isa. xxxii. 5; xxviii. 6; Hag. ii. 5; Zech. iv. 6; vi. 8, etc. See above, p. 5.

[2] A. Dupont-Sommer in R.H.R. 142 (1942), 16–17.

[3] For the beginnings of this in Jewish thought cf. Asc. Isa. iii. 26, 28.

determining a man's whole existence. It is the "Good",
for which he has already declared himself in his pre-
earthly existence, and for which he is continually declaring
himself afresh. Yet he does not think of it just as an
idea, but as a challenging and sustaining power of God.[1]

This is different from Hellenism, for the dualism is felt
as something which permeates both the bodily and the
spiritual world. Thus the *Manual of Discipline* is dominated by the conception of two spirits contending for a man,
one of "truth" and one of "wickedness" (iii. 18–19; iv.
23 ff.).[2] Other names for them are "spirit of light",
"angel of truth", "prince of lights" (this occurs also in
Damascus Document, v. 18; iv. 4), "spirit of knowledge", or
"spirit (or angel) of darkness" (iii. 20–25; iv. 4).[3] The
main significance of this conception is simply to bring out
the element of decision involved in human life; an element
which is similarly brought out in the Old Testament
(where the choice is between Yahweh and Baal) or in the
Rabbis (where it is between Good and Evil). Thus when
the *Manual of Discipline* (iii. 20–21) talks of "walking in
them" (i.e. the two spirits), this means simply "walking
in the ways of light" or "of darkness". The "counsels"
of the good spirit lay upon one a whole series of virtues,
while a list of vices enumerates what belongs to the "spirit
of wickedness". Yet there is an emphasis here, which is
stronger than in the Rabbinic analysis and is closer to the
Old Testament, on man living (or else succumbing to
evil) not by his own strength but by that of God.[4] In
contrast to the Persian system, it is firmly believed that

[1] "The 'holy spirit' is at one moment an aspect of the being of Ahura
Mazda, indeed the most characteristic aspect, if not his actual being
itself; at another moment it is an independent being alongside of him."
E. Abegg in Neue Zürcher Zeitung 11th Jan. 1955.

[2] For war between angels and Azazel see Apoc. Abr. 13–14; Philo,
Abr. 13–14; *Plant.* 23–4; between God's angels and devils, Just. *Dial.* cxvi. 1.

[3] In the *War*, xiii. 10–11, the "prince of light" is opposed to the "angel
of hostility".

[4] *Hymns*, iv. 31: "The way of man cannot be established save by the
spirit which God has fashioned for him."

both of the spirits, or angels,[1] were created by God (*M.D.* iii. 25); and the experience of the overwhelming force of evil is consequently expressed by the conception of a large number of evil spirits (*Hymns*, iii. 18; *M.D.* iii. 14; iv. 20).[2] Indeed, there is such a strong realization that man is controlled from outside himself, that many statements come close to a doctrine of predestination.[3]

Alongside of this, the word "spirit" is used in a different way,[4] to mean the "spirit of man"[5] (*M.D.* iv. 3 (?); viii. 3; xi. 1; *Hymns*, i. 8–9; xv. 32; ii. 15). It can then be identical with the pronoun "I" (*Hymns*, iv. 36; vii. 29). On the one hand this means the "understanding" (*M.D.* v. 23–24; vi. 14, 17), on the other hand it includes both understanding and action (v. 21, cf. ii. 20, iv. 26; ix. 14; *Damascus Document* xx. 24). In fact, the word is on the way to meaning: the existence of a man specifically as he lives before God, i.e. the self which is set over his soul and body.[6]

These ideas were further developed in both Jewish (Testament of the 12 Patriarchs[7]) and Christian literature (Hermas).[8] They never became altogether clear concepts, and the confusion is due to another factor of quite

[1] Spirits and angels are synonymous in *War*, xiii. 10–11.

[2] There is a plurality of *good* angels in *War*, xii. 9; xiii. 10; xix. 1; of evil ones, xiii. 2, 11–12; xiv. 10; xv. 13.

[3] *M.D.* iv. 24–5; *Hymns*, iii. 22–3. Cf. *M.D.* iii. 13–14, 24, and iii. 26–iv. 1, which certainly refer to the two spirits.

[4] Apart from "winds" (*Hymns*, i. 10), "messengers of God", etc. (*M.D.*, ix. 3; *Hymns*, xii. 12; xvi. 12).

[5] Though not imprisoned in the body, as Dupont-Sommer, *op. cit.* 32, infers from *M.D.* iv. 20–1. Cf. *War*, vii. 5: "perfect in spirit and flesh (רוח ובשר)"; *Hymns*, ix. 16, where man appears as "flesh" or as "spirit". Cf. I. P. Hyatt, *The View of Man in the Qumran 'Hodayot*, N.T.St. 2 (1955/56), 276–84.

[6] [This point is discussed by W. D. Davies in *The Scrolls and the N.T.* (ed. K. Stendahl) 77.]

[7] Cf. P. A. Munch, *The Spirits in Test. XII*, Acta Orientalia, 13 (1935), 257–63. I disagree with him in regarding the demonic concepts as primary, the psychological concepts (Test. D. ii–iv: "spirit of wrath" = "wrath") as secondary. Against those who regard Test. XII as Jewish–Christian in origin see W. F. Albright in *Background of the N.T. and its Eschatology*, 166. Cf. M. Burrows, *The Dead Sea Scrolls*, 221.

[8] Cf. J. P. Audet, *Affinités littéraires et doctrinales du M.D.*, Rev. Bibl. 59 (1952), 219–38.

independent origin.   Late Judaism already used the God-given "soul" as a name for one's responsible existence before God, and as such had no hesitation in calling this "spirit"; and this brought up the whole question of human responsibility.   The immediate solution was to make another distinction, this time between the "spirit" and the "I" of a man which is able either to preserve or to destroy the "spirit" (*Damascus Document*, v. 11 [vii. 12]; vii. 3–4 [viii. 20]); and usually this "spirit" can be clearly distinguished from the biological life-force (Test. N. x. 9, Hebrew).   On this view the "spirit" was still God-given, and in the last analysis still belonged to God; but it was now conceived of, not as the active agent of ethical decision, but as passively determined by that decision.[1]

At all events, the problem was now being tackled.   It was given a particular twist in Gnosticism; it lies close to the surface throughout the New Testament; and it is given a radical solution in Paul.

c.   Gnosticism

In Hellenistic thought, power is conceived of as a sub-stance.[2]   When Judaism became involved with the old Greek question about the ἀρχή, which was not merely an inquiry into the First Cause of the universe but also into its Essence (which for a Greek meant also the essence of God), only one answer was possible: Yahweh.   To put it in more modern scientific terms, it was necessary to be more specific and say: his Spirit.   This word "spirit" was eminently suitable: it conformed to Old Testament doc-trine; for the Greeks, it included the concept of the "stuff of life"; and in Egypt, the centre of Hellenistic Judaism, it also suggested the age-old image of God's breath entering

---

[1] In Hermas this becomes God's παρακαταθήκη, which can be returned to him either "deceitful", "useless", or else "unspotted", indeed "renewed" (m. III, ii; s. IX, xiv. 3; xxxii. 2–4).

[2] Nemesius, *De natura hominis*, 30 and 40 (M.P.G. xl. 540b, 561a): "Power (δύναμις) is matter (ὕλη τις)", etc. Cf. Diog. L. VII, 56.   See below, p. 56, n. 1.

into matter and giving it life.[1]   And from now on, a new importance was attached to the creative role of the Spirit in Gen. i. 2.[2]

What is new here is that the Spirit is coming to be understood more and more as substance—although no individual would probably be aware how far he was interpreting this concept according either to Old Testament or to Hellenistic thought.   When the Jew talked of the holy "Spirit" in the sense of human psychology, he meant something that was very important to him: the god-given spiritual existence of man.   But to the Hellenist, this could only evoke the image of the soul which is imprisoned in the body,[3] having descended from the realm of God and ready to ascend thither again after death.   Indeed in the Hellenistic period the unity between God and the world tended to fall further and further apart.   The contrast between the heavenly realm of light and the material world was sensed more and more acutely.   The soul was felt increasingly to be alien, though of the same substance as God.

It was this kind of attitude towards the world which produced a longing for the Golden Age, which once existed and will one day come again.   In Judaism the Paradise story began to take on new significance.   Adam, as the divine First Man, played an ever more important part.   Two notions consequently gained currency in Judaism—one of a heavenly Being who had "fallen" in the First Age, the other of a "Man" who would come in the Last Age.   This myth of a fallen divine First Man was then combined with the Greek soul-myth, a combination

---

[1] Diod. S. I, xii. 1–2; Plut. *Is. et Os.* 36. Cf. Eichrodt, *Theologie des A.T.*[3] II, 19; G. Verbeke, *L'évolution de la doctrine du pneuma*, 335–7.

[2] Herm. s. V, vi. 5; C.H. i. 5; iii. 1 (C. H. Dodd, *The Bible and the Greeks*, 101–34, 217–31; Verbeke, *op. cit.* 318–19); Ascl. 14. Gnostics: Iren. *Haer.* I, xxx. 1; Hipp. *Ref.* V. xix. 13–19, cf. x. 2; Epiph. *Haer.* 25. v. 1; Ps-Clem. *Hom.* XI, 22–4.

[3] Seneca, *Dialogi* XII, vi. 7; *Epistulae Morales*, lxvi. 12; Porphyrius, *Sententiae*, 29 (ed. B. Mommert, 1907), C.H. xxvi. 13 (Nock-Fest. IV, lxxxv. 3 ff.).

which may have been facilitated by the fact that the old Greek gods had now been given new characters as symbols for the Logos, i.e. the divine part of man. Myths about the gods began to be interpreted as representations of the destiny of the soul, which in turn acquired mythical forms. When the Church preached Jesus as the "Man" of the Last Age who had now come, Hellenists could only see in this the return of the fallen First Man, i.e. the "Second Adam". In Jesus' descent and ascension they saw the destiny of the individual soul, perhaps even encouraged to do so by the Church's conception, taken over from the mystery-religions, that the faithful themselves relive the destiny of God.

However, it appeared to follow from Isa. xxxi. 3 that the divine world is characterized by spirit, and the human world by flesh ($\sigma \acute{\alpha} \rho \xi$).[1] In a Hellenistic context, this could only be understood as a proposition about substances. The "Man" (or Son of Man) is he in whom the original heavenly substance has once more made its entry into the material world in order to free its kindred soul-substance in man, that it may rise into its own original heavenly home. But in that case, how can God and his Spirit be the creator of matter, which in itself is evil?[2] How can there be a divine Spirit in material man?

Gnosticism attempts to answer this question in a great variety of ways.[3] The nature of God is spiritual.[4] At

---

[1] Cf. Num. xvi. 22; xxvii. 16, where the LXX separates the realm of the spirits from the realm of flesh by altering "God of the spirits of all flesh" to "God of the spirits *and* all flesh". (Similarly 1 Clem. lix. 3; lxiv; Ditt. Syll.³ III, 1181, 2–3.)

[2] This possibility is radically denied by Cerinthus (Iren. *Haer.* I, xxxvi. 1) and the Manichaeans (Acta Archelai, 7). Irenaeus (*Haer.* II, iii. 2) wrestles with the blasphemy that "the world could be a product of the Fall and of ignorance".

[3] Here we attempt only to give the broadest outlines. Necessary distinctions of detail have to be omitted. For Valentine's school, see the excellent detailed treatment by F. Sagnard, *La gnose valentinienne et le témoignage de St. Irenée* (1946).

[4] Heracleon fr. 24 (Orig. *Comm. in Joh.* xiii. 25); cf. C.H. xviii. 3. For parallels in Egyptian religion: Plut. *Is. et Os.* xxxvi (II, 365d); *Quaest. Conv.* VIII. 1 (II, 718ab); Diod. S. I, xii. 2; cf. Verbeke, *op. cit* 292.

the creation, a spiritual substance [1] is in some way [2] united with matter and yearns for release. [3] Occasionally it may be referred to as "soul", ψυχή, [4] or λογικὴ ψυχή, [5] but mostly the spirit as the divine self is explicitly distinguished from the earthly soul, [6] since it is of the same nature as God or as Christ. [7] This is particularly evident in Valentine. Here, the "seed" or "embryo" (σπέρμα τῆς ἄνωθεν οὐσίας, κύημα or σπέρμα πνευματικόν), which has the same kind of existence as the angels, is mixed with the soul by the Redeemer, unknown to the Demiurge. [8] But this seed is "put to death by existence in the world": all that remains alive is its alter-ego, the "angel", [9] which however only exists since the time of Christ, for he is none other than the Christ who enters each individual. [10] This whole mythology simply represents a concern to separate the spirit, as the substance which is a gift of grace and cannot be lost, from the other two constituents of man, soul and body. [11] It follows that in Gnostic thought Redemption is nothing other than the reassembly of all the sparks of the Spirit. It is effected by the Redeemer, whose nature is spiritual, descending into matter, collecting the spiritual fragments, and reascending with them. [12] His ascension is the beginning of the separating-out process

[1] πνευματικὴ οὐσία (Iren. *Haer.* I, ii. 4). Cf. Sagnard, *op. cit.* 398–415.
[2] Basileides even tries to bring *creatio ex nihilo* into a gnostic system. (G. Quispel in Eranos Jbch., 16 (1948), 120–1).
[3] Cl. Al. *Strom.* IV, xxvi. 3–4; Heracleon, fr. 23 (Orig. *Comm. in Joh.* xiii. 20); Hipp. *Haer.* V, x. 2; xix. 16; xxvi. 17; Acta Archelai, 8.
[4] E.g. Hipp. *Haer.* V, x. 2; Pistis Sophia 111, 132. Acta Archelai, 8.
[5] Cl. Al. *Strom.* II, xx. 112.
[6] Iren. *Haer.* I, xxi. 4; cf. Hipp. *Haer.* V, xxvi. 8, 25; VI, xxxiv. 1; VII xxvii. 6.
[7] Heracleon, fr. 24 (Orig. *Comm. in Joh.* xiii. 25); Odes of Solomon (ed. Rendel Harris), xxvi. 6–7; Iren. *Haer.* I, v. 6: ὁμοούσιον τῇ μητρί (id est Σοφία).
[8] Iren. *Haer.* I, iv. 5; v. 6; II, xix. 1, 3; Cl. Al. *Strom.* II, xxxvi. 2–3; IV, xc. 3–4; *Exc. Theod.* ii; liii. 2–5.
[9] Cl. Al. *Exc. Theod.* xxii. 2; Heracleon, fr. 35 (Orig. *Comm. in Joh.* xiii. 49).
[10] Cl. Al. *Exc. Theod.* xxxvi. 1–2.
[11] "The spiritual element is not nature, but grace", Tertull. *Val.* 29; Quispel, *op. cit.* 262–7, 274–5.
[12] Cl. Al. *Exc. Theod.* xlii. 2; Eus. *Hist. Eccl.* I, xiii. 20; Acta Archelai, 8.

3

by which he gives his body and soul to chaos and his Spirit back to God.[1] Like him, the redeemed also turn into pure spirits by being freed from all ties of body and soul.[2] As soon as they are all once more gathered into the great Spiritual Body,[3] redemption is complete. Despite the mythical imagery, the descent and ascension of the Redeemer is in the end only a paradigm of the destiny of the Spirit that is tied to man. Whether it is thought of as a historical event is immaterial.[4] One way or another, it serves only to remind[5] the spiritual man of the imperishable substance which lives within him, whose nature it is to be saved ($\phi\acute{u}\sigma\epsilon\iota$ $\sigma\omega\zeta\acute{o}\mu\epsilon\nu os$).[6] In the last analysis, the Redeemer is none other than the Spiritual Man himself.[7]

Thus Spirit is separated from soul, and the three-fold division of man into body, soul and an added, God-given spirit is clear and complete.[8] In Greek literature there existed already the Platonic three-fold division[9] and the later triad of mind-soul-body.[10] But this was not a real trichotomy: the mind was not separated from the body.[11]

[1] Hipp. *Haer.* V, xxvi. 31–2; VII, xxxvii. 10–12; Cl. Al. *Exc. Theod.* i. 1–2.

[2] Iren. *Haer.* I, vii. 1 (cf. xxi. 5); Cl. Al. *Exc. Theod.* lxiv.

[3] Acta Joh. 100. Evidence in Büchsel, *Kommentar zu den Johannesbriefen* (1933), 285, n. 1.

[4] Cf. Quispel, *op. cit.* 249–50. It therefore remains open to question whether or not the Gnostic Redeemer-figure is pre-Christian.

[5] Act. Thom. 110; Cl. Al. *Paed.* I, xxxii. 1; cf. Iren. *Haer.* I, iv. 1; viii. 2.

[6] Iren. *Haer.* I, vi. 2; Cl. Al. *Strom.* II, x. 2; IV, lxxxix. 4; V, iii. 3; *Exc. Theod.* lvi. 3.

[7] "Le point de départ est toujours l'homme" (Sagnard, *op. cit.* 568). On all this, see R. Bultmann's article in Kittel s.v. $\gamma\iota\nu\acute{\omega}\sigma\kappa\omega$, E. T. *Gnosis*, 7–14; R. P. Casey, 'Gnosis, Gnosticism and the *N.T.*', in *The Background of the N.T. and its Eschatology* (1956), 52–80; W. F. Albright, *Discoveries in Palestine and the Gospel of St. John, ibid.* 162–3.

[8] Iren. *Haer.* I, v. 6; vi. 1. Correspondingly there are three classes of men, vii. 5. Further instances in Sagnard, *op. cit.* 172–98.

[9] *Phaedrus*, 247c; *Rep.* VI, 508d; taken over by e.g. Philo, *Leg. All.* I, xxii–xxiii.

[10] For Aristotle and Plutarch, see E. B. Allo, R.B. 43 (1934), 335. Also M. Ant. XII, iii. 1 (cf. xiv. 5); V, xxxiii. 6; VIII, lvi. 1–2; II, ii. 1.

[11] In his general appraisal, Burton (*Spirit, Soul and Flesh*, 205–7) does not allow for the fact that there are no Greek parallels to the superiority of $\pi\nu\epsilon\hat{u}\mu\alpha$ over $\psi\upsilon\chi\acute{\eta}$ which may not have been influenced by Judaism or Christianity. The same goes for magic texts (cf. Verbeke, *op. cit.* 322–37).

By contrast, the concept of the Spirit of God standing over against the body and soul of man is central in Judaism, and is applied also to the Spirit which dwells in man. The transition is particularly clear in Irenaeus, where the Spirit of God is grasped as the power which resurrects body and soul.[1] while at the same time it is maintained that man is only perfect when the Spirit is added to body and soul.[2] The Jew is aware that in the Old Testament the soul belongs to the flesh,[3] but he also wishes to portray the natural man as one who thinks, and wills, and lives a conscious life. Therefore when he wants to talk about the opposite of "spiritual" he may just as well say "of the soul" (ψυχικός) as "of the body" (σωματικός).[4] Since this opposition of spirit and soul has so far only been found in literature which is either Jewish or Christian or else influenced by them, it appears that the decisive conception must have been the Jewish one of the Spirit which both transcends a man and dwells within him.[5]

[1] *Epid.* xlii. Also Mart. Polycarpi xiv. 2 (Eus. *Hist. Eccl.* IV, xv. 34).

[2] Iren. *Haer.* V, vi. 1. Also Cl. Al. *Strom.* V, lxxxvii. 4–lxxxviii. 4; Tat. *Or. Graec.* xv. 2.

[3] Eth. Enoch, xvi. 1: "flesh-soul"; J. A. T. Robinson, *The Body* (1952), 23, n. 2. Yet this use of words cannot be derived from Gen. ii. 7 (R. Bultmann, *Gnosis*, J.T.S. (N.S.), 3 (1952), 14–16).

[4] E.g. Epiph. *Haer.* 33, v. 13, or σαρκικός Ign. *Eph.* vii. 2; x. 3; *Sm.* xii. 2; xiii. 2; *Mag.* xiii. 2; *Pol.* i. 2; ii. 2. See below, p. 87.

[5] See above, p. 17. Cf. Allo, *op. cit.* 336–41; Verbeke, *op. cit.* 538–43.

THE NEW TESTAMENT

LONG before the Spirit was an article of doctrine it was a fact in the experience of the primitive Church. This explains why the New Testament statements about it exhibit both such diversity and such unity.

A. MARK AND MATTHEW

1. *Demonic and psychological "spirit"*

Out of 23 occurrences of the word spirit ($\pi\nu\epsilon\hat{\upsilon}\mu\alpha$) in Mark, 14 are in a phrase like "unclean spirit" ($\pi\nu\epsilon\hat{\upsilon}\mu\alpha$ $\dot{\alpha}\kappa\dot{\alpha}\theta\alpha\rho\tau\sigma\nu$), meaning "demon" ($\delta\alpha\acute{\iota}\mu\omega\nu$ or $\delta\alpha\iota\mu\acute{\sigma}\nu\iota\sigma\nu$) [1]— a concept which is familiar from contemporary Judaism. Matthew usually avoids this term, and in viii. 16 goes to the other extreme when he renders "demons" ($\delta\alpha\iota\mu\acute{\sigma}\nu\iota\alpha$ in Mark i. 34) by "spirits" ($\tau\dot{\alpha}$ $\pi\nu\epsilon\acute{\upsilon}\mu\alpha\tau\alpha$) without any qualifying word.

In Mark ii. 8 "spirit" seems to be purely psychological ("Jesus knowing in his spirit . . .", cf. v. 30 "knowing in himself"); in Mark viii. 12 it is the seat of perception and emotion, and in Matt. xxvii. 50 it is the life-force.

There is a special shade of meaning in Mark xiv. 38, where the "willing spirit" ($\pi\nu\epsilon\hat{\upsilon}\mu\alpha$ $\pi\rho\acute{\sigma}\theta\upsilon\mu\sigma\nu$) is contrasted with the "weak flesh" ($\sigma\grave{\alpha}\rho\xi$ $\dot{\alpha}\sigma\theta\epsilon\nu\acute{\eta}s$). This reflects the experience of a conflict within man, which can already be seen in the *Manual of Discipline* and elsewhere in Hellenistic psychology. It implies that the opposite of (sinful) flesh is not some better part of man's

---

[1] The synoptic parallels to $\pi\nu\epsilon\acute{\upsilon}\mu\alpha\tau\alpha$ $\dot{\alpha}\kappa\dot{\alpha}\theta\alpha\rho\tau\alpha$ in Mark v. 13 are $\delta\alpha\acute{\iota}\mu\sigma\nu\epsilon s$ and $\delta\alpha\iota\mu\acute{\sigma}\nu\iota\alpha$. Cf. E. Langton, *Essentials of Demonology* (1949), 147–71; S. Eitrem, *Some Notes on the Demonology in the N.T.*, Symb. Osl. xxvii. (1950); V. McCasland, *By the finger of God* (1951).

nature, but is the effect of God's will. Once it is realized that the expression "willing spirit" derives from the Hebrew text of Ps. li. 12,[1] where it is identical with the "Holy Spirit" of God, and that here the prayer is for strength in temptation, it becomes clear that what is meant by "spirit" is the Spirit of God which is temporarily imparted to a man and fights against human weakness.

2. *The Spirit as the Power of God*

However, the meaning of "spirit" ($\pi\nu\epsilon\hat{v}\mu\alpha$) in Matthew and Mark is to all intents and purposes determined by the Old Testament concept of God's power to do certain things.[2] The "blasphemy against the Holy Spirit" is committed, according to Mark iii. 28–30, by those who, when Jesus casts out devils, mistake the power of God for the apparently similar[3] power of the devil.

The formation of this *Logion* is hard to determine. In its Marcan form, the blasphemy against the Spirit is contrasted with all other sins and blasphemies, in its Q form only with blasphemy against the Son of Man. Matthew places both versions side by side, Luke adopts only Q. It may be conjectured that a pre-Marcan version had $\tau\hat{\omega}$ $vi\hat{\omega}$ $\tau o\hat{v}$ $\dot{\alpha}\nu\theta\rho\dot{\omega}\pi o v$,[4] which in one tradition turned into the completely unambiguous $\tau o\hat{\iota}s$ $vi o\hat{\iota}s$ $\tau\hat{\omega}\nu$ $\dot{\alpha}\nu\theta\rho\dot{\omega}\pi\omega\nu$ of Mark, and in another, at a time when "Son of Man" was only understood as referring to Jesus,[5] into the Q version. But it is more likely that the saying was originally a missionary slogan, intended to show the Jews the gravity of their decision.[6] There is

[1] Lohmeyer, *Komm. zu Mk. ad loc.*
[2] E.g. Ezek. i. 12, 20; Judges xiii. 25; xiv. 6, 19; xv. 14.
[3] That is why both can still be described as $\pi\nu\epsilon\hat{v}\mu\alpha$, though this usage is avoided more and more. Yet the $\delta\alpha\iota\mu o\nu\iota\zeta\dot{o}\mu\epsilon\nu os$ of the synoptics is never contrasted with the $\pi\nu\epsilon\nu\mu\alpha\tau\iota\kappa\dot{o}s$ of the Epistles as his good counter-part (Jackson-Lake, I, v. 102–3).
[4] Apart from this, the title Son of God hardly occurs in Mark before Peter's confession (T. W. Manson, *The Teaching of Jesus*, 214). See further, Jackson-Lake, I, i. 380–1.
[5] Wellhausen, *Mt., ad loc.*; A. Loisy, *Les évangiles synoptiques, ad loc.* For the fact, cf. Did. xi. 7; II Cor. vii. 2, 17.
[6] The saying can hardly go back to Jesus, despite R.N. Flew, *Jesus and His Church*, 49.

something similar in Acts iii. 17. In its certain knowledge of possessing the Spirit (I Thess. i. 6, etc.) the Church sees the end of the age of uncertainty. The title "Son of Man" in this case denotes the earthly man who is not yet installed as the Son of God κατὰ πνεῦμα (see below, pp. 57–8).

In any case, the *Logion* is evidence for the Church's boundless conviction that it possessed the Spirit. In this connection it is noticeable how in Mark iii. 28 and Matt. xii. 32α[1] it is the incredible magnitude of what is forgiven that is especially emphasized. It is as a corollary to this that one must understand the severity with which resistance to the manifestation of the Spirit is castigated. Granted the Church's conviction of the reality of the Spirit working within it, such resistance could only be regarded as wilfulness against the overpowering force of the Spirit.[2] No forgiveness is available, because none is asked for.[3]

Matt. xii. 28 ("If I, by the Spirit of God, cast out demons . . .") belongs to the same context. "Spirit" (πνεύματι) is presumably a correction by the primitive Church (which had experienced the working of the Spirit in its midst) for the original "finger" (δακτύλῳ Luke xi. 20). Now the Spirit of God does not appear among the various means of casting out devils known to the Rabbis.[4] Therefore this attitude is completely new; and what is remarkable in this passage is that the presence of the Spirit (casting out devils) is interpreted as the presence of the kingdom (βασιλεία).[5] In the same way, the promise that God will put his Spirit upon his Servant is seen to be fulfilled, according to Matt. xii. 18, in Jesus' work of

[1] Matt. xii. 32α is better adapted to a situation after Pentecost, while Mark refers it to an event before Pentecost (iii. 30).

[2] Kittel, art. *Sin*, E.T. 68.

[3] Consequently the saying cannot be addressed to those who are anxious about being guilty of it.

[4] Str.-B. IV, 532–5 (cf. the dramatic casting out of devils in front of Vespasian).

[5] Kittel, art. *Basileia*, E.T. 42. The saying, at least in essentials, may well go back to Jesus.

healing; and this is of a piece with the Church's conviction that with the coming of this miraculous Spirit the
Last Age is breaking in.

There is nothing further to be learnt from Mark i. 12
("immediately the Spirit drove him out ($\dot{\epsilon}\kappa\beta\acute{\alpha}\lambda\lambda\epsilon\iota$) into the
wilderness"), where the Old Testament colouring[1] comes
out so crudely that is already modified in Matthew.
Here, the Spirit is not understood as anything like help in
temptation, but as the irresistible power of God which
goes off with its victim.[2]

3. *General endowment with the Spirit*

It is significant that the Rabbinic identification of the
Holy Spirit with Scripture (see above pp. 28–9) only crops
up once, in Matt. xii. 36.   The Church is conscious that it
has received the prophetic Spirit not only in the past
epoch of salvation—the time of the scriptural prophets—
but also in the present (Mark xiii. 11 and parallels[3]).
The Old Testament view is that the Spirit mediates the
word of God (II Sam. xxiii. 2); but this is now understood
in a different way, in that the utterance of the Spirit is a
sign of God's help in the eschatological time of need.[4]

It is true that a general endowment with the Spirit is
only referred to in Mark i. 8 ("He will baptize you with
the Holy Spirit").   Mark certainly saw the fulfilment
of this saying in the pouring out of the Spirit upon the
Church[5]—which is also the interpretation in Acts (i. 5;
xi. 16).

The Q version is doubtless the more original.   It is
easily understandable that the incomprehensible $\kappa\alpha\grave{\iota}$ $\pi\nu\rho\acute{\iota}$

---

[1] Cf. II Kings ii. 16 (hi. שׁלך); Ezek. viii. 3; xi. 1, 24; xliii. 5 (hi. בוא); Ezek.
xxxvii. 1 (hi. יצא).

[2] See below, p. 44 top.

[3] The form in Q is probably original (Lohmeyer, *Markus*, 273).

[4] The saying which limits endowment with the Spirit to particular times
of need may well be dominical (Loh. *Markus, ad loc.*, W. F. Howard, *Christianity according to St. John*, 78); the replacement of the Spirit by the ascended
Christ and the broadening of the promise (Luke xxi. 15) are secondary.

[5] Did Mark xvi. 9 ff. once recount this? (Barrett, *Gospel Tradition*, 125.)

should have been left out, but not that it should have
been added; for no fire-baptism in fact took place.
Even Luke did not see it happening in Acts ii. 3, since in
i. 5 he only quotes the saying in its Marcan form.   In
this case it must go back to the Baptist (or to Jesus) and
belongs to the circles of intense eschatological expectation.
Fire is a widely-known symbol of judgment,[1] and this
more than anything is its meaning in the verses which
immediately surround this *logion*, viz.: Matt. iii. 10, 12 =
Luke iii. 9, 17 = Q.   Thus baptism by fire,[2] in the oldest
form of the saying which we can trace, was understood as
eschatological judgment.   But in this case "He who
cometh" is surely not only Elijah, but the Messianic
judge.[3]   It is questionable whether this also explains
satisfactorily the promise of a baptism by the Spirit,
or whether this promise was originally a Christian addition.[4]

Eschatological expectations are met by endowment
with the Spirit—often in the imagery of cleansing water [5]
—and also by the Fire of Judgment.   Both appear also in
the Dead Sea Scrolls (*M.D.* iv. 13, 21).   In this case the
Messiah would have the double task of both destroying
the ungodly and of saving the devout.   In fact, however,
the two concepts are not so strictly connected, and the
Messiah is seldom regarded as a dispenser of the Spirit
(see above, p. 11).   Moreover, unless this distinction
were made clear, it would not be easy, within the single
image of judgment, suddenly to conceive both of Spirit
as a gift of grace and of fire as the instrument of judgment.   It is more likely that "spirit" originally meant

[1] Isa. lxvi. 15–16 (cf. i. 31; xxx. 30, 33; xxxi. 9; xxxiv. 9–10); Amos. i. 4;
vii. 4; Mal. iii. 2; Ps. Sol. xv. 4; IV Ezra xiii. 4, 10; Syr. Baruch xlviii. 39;
Test. Abr. 14 (ed. M. R. James, xciv. 18); Mark ix. 43–9; I Cor. iii. 13;
II Thess. i. 8; II Peter. iii. 7; Rev. xx. 9; Qumran, *Hymns*, iii. 28–31; vi. 18;
M.D. ii. 8, 15; iv. 13.
[2] The phrase was formed by analogy to John's water-baptism (C. H.
Kraeling, *John the Baptist*, 114–18).   In Mark x. 38–9, Luke xii. 50,
βαπτισθῆναι is used figuratively.
[3] At most a "Messianic" Elijah: W. H. Brownlee, *John the Baptist in the
New Light of Ancient Scrolls*, Interpretation 9 (1955), 86–7.
[4] See most recently, V. Taylor, *Mark, ad loc.*
[5] T. F. Torrance, *Proselyte Baptism*, N.T.St. 1 (1954–5) 152–3.   Schlatter,
Joh. on iii. 5.

"wind".[1] Storm-wind and fire are often mentioned together, e.g. in the description of the "Son of Man" who comes to the judgment on the clouds of heaven.[2] And in particular, both are presupposed in the immediately adjacent sentence in Matthew (iii. 12): the winnowing is done in the storm-wind (Isa. xli. 16; cf. xxvii. 12; Jer. iv. 11; Amos. ix. 9) and the chaff is consumed with fire.[3]

If then the baptism of John was originally understood as the rite by which a throng of penitents hoped to escape imminent judgment,[4] a decisive step forward was made by the Synoptics' understanding of it: having a share in the Spirit in the Church of Jesus is already an anticipation of salvation from the eschatological judgment. Baptism "by Spirit and Fire" has become the fulfilment of the saving function of John's baptism. It is still understood as judgment by separation and purification; but this is no longer merely awaited in the future: it is experienced in the present—experienced, that is, as salvation for all who submit to it.

4. Jesus' endowment with the Spirit at his Baptism

The account of Jesus' baptism is preserved only in the form which it has in Mark i. 9 ff.[5] Even this is an account of something other than the call of a prophet. Of all the possibilities, the most likely is that this is an account of the

---

[1] As frequently in the O.T. Cf. Barrett, *Gospel Tradition*, 126; Kraeling, *op. cit.* 63; Taylor, *Mark, ad loc.* (as a possibility).

[2] IV Ezra xiii. 10, 27 (spiritus, ignis, tempestas). Cf. Isa. xxix. 6; xxx. 27; Ezek. i. 4, etc. In particular, in Gen. R. 83, the judgment of the heathen is compared with winnowing, helped by fire (Mal. iii. 19) and storm-wind (Isa. xli. 16).

[3] M. Goguel, in Rev. H. Ph. R. 5 (1925), 68, sees the influence of this saying in Rev. xiv. 14–20 (18 πυρός).

[4] Kraeling, *op. cit.* 118–22; Barrett, *Gospel Tradition*, 31–4.

[5] Matt. iv. 3α, 6α suggests that Q already knew of a proclamation of the Son of God. Against the view that the story is a cult-legend (A. Loisy, *Luc, ad loc.*), must be set the lack of an institution-narrative (as in Matt. xxviii. 19); against the view that it is a Baptist-legend proving Jesus' inferiority (M. Goguel in Rev. H. Ph. R. 13 (1933), 424, n. 13), the total withdrawal of the Baptist and the voice from heaven. πνεῦμα used absolutely is not necessarily Hellenistic (*M.D.* iv. 6; *War*, vii. 6?), and "son" for "king" certainly not.

gift of the Spirit to the Messiah. The Messiah has the Spirit of God: that is an Old Testament promise which is repeated in Judaism (see above p. 11);[1] and that this event is quite different from anything in the prophets is made explicit (apart from the visible apparition of the dove and the audible testimony of God), not through any new doctrine of the Spirit,[2] but through the fact that *this* gift of the Spirit takes place at the End of the Age, after a long period when the Spirit was extinct (see above p. 13).[3] In this way the event is pin-pointed as the beginning of the new Divine Age. For this reason also it is in a completely different class from Hellenistic accounts of ecstatic phenomena.[4] The original significance of the gift of the Spirit in Baptism is that it marks the beginning of Messiahship; but, unlike later Adoptianism, this is not a doctrinal proposition which excludes other possibilities.[5] No difficulty is felt at this stage about the place of the story alongside that of the miraculous conception by the Spirit. It is not a question of giving concrete form to the appearance of a Wonder Man; both stories are concerned to announce the already accepted uniqueness of Jesus by recounting God's direct intervention at certain points in his life. This is their way of saying that, in Jesus, God himself is at work.

5. *Passages peculiar to Matthew*

The first of these to be mentioned is Matt. v. 3. οἱ πτωχοὶ τῷ πνεύματι cannot mean those who are poor in the Holy Spirit. But it is also impossible to take πνεύματι as an instrumental dative. It must be a dative of

---

[1] Barrett, *Gospel Tradition*, 42–4.

[2] No acts of the Spirit are presupposed beyond those in the passages mentioned.

[3] In Judaism, when individuals appear in possession of the Spirit, they too are regarded as a sign of the Last Age.

[4] These are self-induced and remain a private experience of the individual, not a sign of a new act of God. εἰς αὐτόν means no more than ἐπ᾽ αὐτόν (Bl.-Debr. §207, Mark iii. 13, unlike Gosp. Hebr. iv).

[5] Unlike Just. *Dial.* 87–8.

respect,[1] parallel to καθαροὶ τῇ καρδίᾳ and the Rabbinic phrase שפל רוח (Prov. xxix. 23; Isa. lvii. 15). πνεῦμα therefore signifies the human spirit. However, what is new in this, as against the parallels from Judaism,[2] is that this disposition is not demanded as a virtue to be acquired by men, but rather those men are esteemed to whom it is given. Nevertheless, just as "spirit" (רוח) in Judaism was continually taking on more overtones of the religious individuality of man (see above, p. 17), so Matt. v. 3 esteems blessed the poor "people of the land" (אם הארל) who put their whole trust in God, as opposed not so much to those who are materially (Luke vi. 20, 24) or intellectually rich, but to those who are rich in religious knowledge and practice.

A special place belongs to the command to baptize in Matt. xxviii. 19.

It is open to question whether the triple formula may not be an ancient interpolation.[3] Eusebius, 21 times out of 25, quotes it without the formula, and quotes the triple formula only after Nicaea. Justin (*Ap.* I, 61) supports baptism in the triple name with Isa. i. 16 ff. and the apostolic tradition, but does *not* cite Matt. xxviii. 19. In the practice of the Church, the formula appears for the first time in Didache vii. 1. On the other hand, Didache ix. 5 shows that at the same time the single formula was still current. It may be that since it was not based on any particular Trinitanian doctrine, it could crop up from time to time without being felt as anything sensationally new—just as triadic formulae occasionally appear in Paul. Therefore it is not impossible for the time of Matthew.[4] But it cannot go back to Jesus; for Luke, John, Paul and even Mark xvi. 15 have no knowledge of it, and the primitive church knows of no triple formula, nor indeed of any commission to the Gentiles.[5]

---

[1] Bl.-Debr. § 197—exactly as in Ps. xxxiv. 19 (LXX). Qumran, *War*, xi. 9–13 is very instructive: "those who are bruised in spirit" or "the poor" are those who are fighting on God's side: cf. xiii. 14; xiv. 7. Other references in A. Dupont-Sommer, R.H.R. 148 (1955), 160, n. 4.

[2] Str.-B. *ad loc.*

[3] Barrett, *Gospel Tradition*, 102–3.

[4] So A. H. McNeile, *The Gospel acc. to St. Matthew, ad loc.*

[5] Cf. Flemington, *N.T. Doctrine of Baptism*, 108.

What is astonishing about this is not the reference to the Spirit at baptism (see below p. 50), so much as the naming of the Spirit's name (ὄνομα τοῦ πνεύματος) alongside the other two names. This means that here πνεῦμα is understood in a completely different sense from that in any other passage in Matthew. Matthew must have known the formula already as a baptismal formula (perhaps in a very restricted circle). Once the "Lord", κύριος, was placed next to God, it would have been very easy for the Spirit to be added. This did not involve speculation over their mutual relationship; it was rather a proof that God cannot be demonstrated as the apex of a monotheistic system, but can only be encountered when he meets the Church in person: in the Son, or else (for the individual) in the Spirit, in which this encounter with the Son takes place.[1]

6. *The supernatural conception of Jesus by the Spirit*

Finally, Matt. i. 18, 20 must be mentioned: the reference to Jesus' conception.

> This tradition is secondary to that of Luke, since it presupposes polemical opposition to it. The episode is not narrated, but simply reported by the angel to allay a suspicion. An analysis of Luke gives the following results: (1) The Baptist stories were originally independent and nowhere allude to Jesus; (2) the Christmas story does not presuppose i. 26–38. In an attempt at harmonization, Baptist and Jesus stories are woven together, so that they run parallel, and yet give precedence to the Jesus stories (most noticeable in i. 26–38). The most likely conclusion seems to me to be: (a) i. 26–38, ii. 1–20 were originally independent legends; (b) Luke or his predecessor uses them to provide a parallel and to emulate the already current Baptist stories; (c) this motive affects the tradition behind i. 26–38 right from the start, making the parallels clearer here than in ii. 1–20.

[1] It is true that it is impossible to distinguish sharply between liturgical formulae and creeds (but see O. Cullmann, *Early Christian Creeds*, p. 36 n.1.); but this does not mean that formulations of this kind could not have existed before there were any literary examples of triple credal forms.

In Matt. i. 18, 20, as in Luke i. 35, πνεῦμα is the divine creative power, creating the life of this unique child—a conception which we certainly cannot find in Rabbinic Judaism,[1] though we can find it in popular writings.[2] Now it may be that the creative intervention of God in the process of conception was currently believed in, in which case it was but a short step to Luke i. 35 and Matt. i. 20. However, the ground had also been prepared from another direction. In Egyptian-Hellenistic Judaism Isa. vii. 14 had once been interpreted in the sense of a miracle of fatherless birth; furthermore, it is precisely in Egypt that the notion of conception through the Spirit of God was developed; finally, a mass of parallels from comparative religion show that some kind of divine conception was regarded, especially in contemporary Hellenism, as an absolutely indispensable characteristic of the Saviour.[3]

The result was a combination of the belief in a unique example of the creative intervention of God, with the concept (already explicit in the Old Testament) of the creative power of God's Spirit[4]—a concept, which, through Graeco-Egyptian parallels, was applied in Hellenistic Judaism to the process of conception.

7. *Recapitulation*

One conclusion from this survey is that Matthew and Mark contain astoundingly few statements about the Spirit. Only one of these (Matt. xiii. 11 and parallels) or the gist of it, can be attributed with any certainty to Jesus. This shows, in the first place, the astonishing fidelity of the tradition: the early Church's experiences of

---

[1] Indeed, our story is told in order to outbid the story of the direct intervention of God at the birth of John, for which parallels can be found in Str.-B. I, 49–50.

[2] See above, p. 14.

[3] In Philo (*Cher.* 40–52; *Fug.* 108–9; *Ebr.* 30; *Leg. All.* ii. 49–51, on which see Barrett, *Gospel Tradition*, 9–10) the mythical background of Egyptian thought is still visible. For Philo himself the event is purely spiritual. See Barrett, *Gospel Tradition*, 10–15, on other lines of interpretation.

[4] Cf. Barrett, *Gospel Tradition*, 17–24.

the Spirit have hardly been read back at all into the description of Jesus' life.[1] There is also, however, a significant theological point to be considered.

The temptation to portray Jesus as a Man of the Spirit must have been considerable. Even if Jesus did not betray many of the marks of ecstatic piety, nevertheless, even under critical analysis, the tradition about him still has quite a large "spiritual" element compared with anything in Rabbinic literature. Thus even the references to his power (ἐξουσία, δύναμις) are really only a variation on the popular and Old Testament sense of "Spirit". Why then is the Spirit mentioned so little? Reference to Isaiah and Jeremiah[2] does not help, since the relevant passages represent a reaction to the abuses of the *Nebiim*; but Jesus does not compete with such figures, even though they occasionally did make their appearance in Judaism. Another possible explanation[3] is that Jesus was originally portrayed as a Man of the Spirit, but that these traits were subsequently suppressed in the interests of a more advanced Christology. But this is an unlikely hypothesis. After all, Judaism knew that the Messiah would be a bearer of the Spirit; so that an accretion of clearly Messianic characteristics might have been expected, but not the suppression of "spiritual" ones. Again, the suggestion that the Spirit, being an "intermediary", would make God seem more distant, while Jesus was proclaiming the direct nearness of the Father,[4] does not work; for it is precisely in the Spirit that the Church experiences the presence of God. Finally, it makes the facts no clearer to say that the presence of the Spirit was so manifest that there was no need for anything to be said about it; for the gospels are not concerned just with settling

[1] R. N. Flew, *Jesus and his Church*, 49; Barrett, in J.T.S. (N.S.) 1 (1950), 1. Flemington, *op. cit.* 95, makes the same point for baptism.

[2] J. E. Fison, *The Blessing of the Holy Spirit*, ch. 5. Barrett, *Gospel Tradition*, 152, is sound on this.

[3] Windisch, *Syn. Ueberlieferung*, 230–4.

[4] E. F. Scott, *The Spirit in the N.T.*, 79.

doubtful points:[1] they report and proclaim. Moreover, Acts and Paul speak constantly about the Spirit.

Therefore it may be taken as a historical fact that Jesus himself said hardly anything about the Spirit.[2] This may have been because he thought of himself at first as Messiah-designate; or else because it was only after the completion of his ministry that his disciples were ready for it;[3] or again because he simply did not expect an out-pouring of the Spirit.[4] But at least in this respect the Johannine view is confirmed (see below p. 96) which bases the full understanding of Jesus, not on his sayings, but on the post-resurrection proclamation of the Church. It was this Church which experienced the gift of the Spirit as a divine sign marking it out as the People of the Last Age. It knew, of course, that this was dependent on the coming of Jesus and on faith in him; but it was a long time before it reached a clear formulation of this belief (see below pp. 54 ff.). On the other hand, the fact that the Church so consistently avoided portraying Jesus simply as the first Man of the Spirit, throws into startlingly high relief its conviction that the role intended for it by Jesus was neither that of being an example of the "spiritual" life, nor the teacher of the People of the Last Age. The only important point was that God encountered his people in Christ. Therefore all that is said about Jesus and the Spirit only underlines Jesus' uniqueness, his "eschatological" status, the fact that God is really present in him as he is nowhere else.[5] This is the purport of the small number of passages

[1] Barrett, *Gospel Tradition*, 141–2.
[2] For another view, see W. F. Lofthouse in Exp. Times, 52 (1940–1), 334–6.
[3] Flew, *op. cit.*, 51.
[4] So Barrett in Exp. Times, 67 (1955–6), 142–5. Some scholars (e.g. Leisegang, Bultmann (*T.N.T.* I, 41), Goguel) attribute the experience of the Spirit to the Hellenistic church.
[5] The position is the exact opposite of that in Judaism, where only the Good Men of the Last Age occupy a central position, and the Messiah, as their mediator, is of secondary importance (Bousset-Gressmann, 222–3). The statement about possession of the Spirit is much less firmly rooted in the early Kerygma than that about the Messiah, cf. C. H. Dodd, *The Apostolic Preaching* (1936), 133–5 = (1944), 57–8.

which portray Jesus as the bearer of "spiritual" power (Matt. xii. 18, 28; Mark iii. 29–30), and still more distinctly of those other passages which, on account of the activity of the Spirit in Jesus, lift him right above his predecessors (Matt. i. 20; Mark i. 10) or describe him as the eschatological Spirit-baptist (Mark i. 8, cf. xiii. 11).

Matthew and Mark therefore have substantially the same conception of the Spirit of God as the Old Testament. Words and deeds which would otherwise lie outside human capacity are made possible by the power of God. Only once (in the notion of the Spirit's part in the conception of Jesus) do more modern ideas from Hellenistic Judaism make their appearance. But what is completely new is the strict subordination of Spirit episodes to the conviction that in them the messianic Last Age has dawned.[1] All statements about the nature of the Spirit are there purely for their Christological importance.

B. Luke and Acts

That the Spirit received a new importance in these circles can be seen at once from the fact that πνεῦμα, as the term for the divine Spirit, is used at least three times as often in Luke as it is in Mark.[2] As for Acts i–xii, which has 37 πνεῦμα-passages, this is relatively the highest incidence in the New Testament.[3] Moreover, it appears from the material that Luke has a new conception of the Spirit. Usually this is regarded as "influence from Greek Asia Minor".[4] But it will become clear that the development was strongly moulded by Judaism. Our method

---

[1] Barrett, *Gospel Tradition*, 153.

[2] πνεῦμα ἀκάθαρτον, etc.: 12 times. For psychological πνεῦμα see below, p. 54.

[3] Acts xiii–xxviii has only 18 instances, although it is about a third longer than i–xii.

[4] E.g. by P. Volz. *Der Geist Gottes*, 198; but it would be hard to imagine the Palestinian Church as "unspiritual". Cf. E. F. Scott, *The Varieties of N.T. Religion*, 32–3; C. C. Torrey, *The Aramaic Period of the Nascent Christian Church*, Z.N.W. 44 (1952–3), 207–8.

will be to start in each case from Luke (since Luke shows most clearly the progress of the concept compared to Mark) and then to complete the picture from Acts.

1. *The relationship between the Spirit and Jesus*

Mark i. 12 runs: "The Spirit cast him out into the wilderness", τὸ πνεῦμα αὐτὸν ἐκβάλλει εἰς τὸν ἐρημόν. Contrast the version in Luke iv. 1: "Jesus being full of the Holy Spirit returned . . . and was led in the Spirit into the wilderness", ἤγετο ἐν τῷ πνεύματι ἐν τῷ ἐρήμῳ. In other words, Luke avoids giving the impression that the Spirit is an agent set over Jesus. He is not satisfied with the Old Testament idea of the power of God falling upon a man (see above p. 4). Instead, Jesus becomes the agent—"in the Holy Spirit".[1] He is no longer a Man of the Spirit, but is now Lord of the Spirit. In iv. 14, Luke introduces the Spirit again, and from then on the dominant description of Jesus is that of one who possesses the power of the Spirit.[2] iv. 18 also (peculiar to Luke) emphasizes the resting of the Spirit upon Jesus. There is a notable reinterpretation in xii. 10, where Luke takes the saying about the sin against the Holy Spirit out of the context which it has in Mark,[3] for the reason that it is impossible for him to see the decisive manifestation of the Spirit in the casting out of demons by the Man of the Spirit, Jesus. ii. 40 is completely parallel to i. 80; but a growing "in the Spirit" is not attributed to

[1] Jesus is led "in" (not "by") the Spirit. πλήρης, as opposed to πλησθείς, indicates being continually full. This is the first instance of the Spirit being a power in the struggle against Satan (G. W. H. Lampe, *The Holy Spirit in the writings of St. Luke*, in *Studies in the Gospels*, ed. Nineham, 170).

[2] Lampe, *op. cit.* 170–1. Luke iv. 14β, 15, describe this possession. Thus it would be wrong to interpret these passages, "on an impulse of the Spirit".

[3] See above, p. 25. It is unlikely that this was already so in Q; for Matt. is not aware of this connection, and Luke xii. 10α, when compared with xii. 9, can hardly be original (although the phraseology, with its asymmetrical πᾶς ὅς . . . , ὁ δέ . . . or τῷ δέ . . . is exactly similar). In any case Luke avoids the interpretation (which he must have known) given in Mark iii. 30. See below p. 41.

4

Jesus as it is to the Baptist.[1]   On the other hand, Luke is able to accept the story of the conception of Jesus by the Spirit, i. 35 (see above, p. 32).   Here, still more than in Matthew, the Spirit appears as the life-begetting creative power of God;[2] but only the event is important, not the manner of its happening: as one born of the Spirit, Jesus, right from the start, is in possession of the Spirit, and not only (like a Man of the Spirit) an object of its activity.   It is no objection to this, that Luke accepts the tradition of the gift of the Spirit at Jesus' baptism (iii. 22),[3] that he records Jesus being filled with the Spirit before an inspired utterance (x. 21),[4] or that he places the final reception of the Spirit after the Ascension (Acts ii. 33).   No phased programme of growth in the Spirit is implied in this; for there stands behind it the Biblical recollection[5] that even when the Spirit is given to a man it is still God's Spirit, so that every time it is active there is ultimately a new act of God (see below, p. 40 n. 2).   That the baptism in the Jordan and the Pentecost story are in no way assimilated to each other is an indication that for Luke the gift of the Spirit to Jesus is on an altogether different level from the gift to the Church.

On the one hand, Jesus is in full possession of the Spirit from the beginning.   On the other hand, after the Resurrection, he is also, for the Church, the donor of the Spirit (Luke xxiv. 49; Acts ii. 33).[6]   This must explain the

---

[1] Lampe, *op. cit.* 168.   The *insertion* of τὸ πνεῦμά μου into the O.T. sequence (i. 47) shows that although πνεῦμα is here interchangeable with ψυχή, nevertheless Luke wishes to emphasize that it is not simply a human faculty which is the agent here, but the self which ultimately cannot be separated from God's Spirit and is bestowed on man.   The same goes for i. 80 and ii. 40.

[2] The pattern Creation/New Creation can hardly be alluded to (despite C. F. Burney, *The Aramaic Origin of the Fourth Gospel*, 44, 47, who sees Christ as the new Adam in i. 78–9; ii. 32; iii. 38).

[3] Indeed, he emphasizes it even more strongly than Mark and Matt.

[4] In Luke x. 21 it is πνεῦμα ἅγιον, whereas πνεῦμα αὐτοῦ of Mark ii. 8 (viii. 12) is not adopted.

[5] See above, p. 2.

[6] The underlying tradition holds (unlike Luke) that the Spirit was first received by the Ascended One (cf. John xx. 22; Eph. iv. 7–12; and the fixing of Ascensiontide in the ancient Eastern Church on the fiftieth day).

growth of the idea that the risen Lord himself is encountered in this his gift, so that either the Spirit or the risen Lord can be referred to interchangeably (compare Luke xii. 12 with xxi. 15, Acts x. 14 with 19 and xvi. 7).

Luke therefore has made a clear theological decision. Mark and Matthew could still naïvely describe Jesus as a "Man of the Spirit", even though at the same time they were evidently already trying to present him as the unique eschatological saviour. Luke has brought this insight into the open: Jesus is not a "Man of the Spirit" in the sense in which men of the Spirit exist in the Church, nor is he an agent of that Spirit which is at work also in the Church. In Jesus, God's Spirit is made manifest for the very first time; it is through Jesus that the Spirit is given to the Church.

2. The "abiding" of the Spirit in the Church

An analogy to all this can be established with reference to the Church. Here again, Luke is trying to rise superior to the concept of the Spirit as a power which at one leap overtakes a man and subsequently abandons him.[1] Typical of this is the fact that alongside the originally animistic concept of the Spirit as an independent being which seizes upon a man and yet is alien from him, there now appears the originally dynamic conception of it as a fluid which fills a man.[2] This conception is better adapted for describing a spirit which leaves its mark on a man's whole existence. At the same time the Gnostic danger is avoided: the Spirit is not automatically a possession of the believer. Thus Luke not only preserves the terminology of the "animistic" conception (since this underlines the divinity of the Spirit, its complete separateness from man); but even when he uses a "dynamic" expression, we find,

[1] Cf. Gen. xli. 38; Num. xi. 17; xxvii. 18; Isa. xlii. 1; lxi. 1; Zeph. iii. 4, LXX; Hos. ix. 7.
[2] The first is mainly in the O.T., the second in Hellenism. Evidence for both in Bultmann, *T.N.T.* I, 155–6. Cf. J. E. L. Oulton, *Holy Communion and Holy Spirit*, 42–8.

besides the phrase "full of the Spirit", πλήρης πνεύματος
(which emphasises the abiding association with the
Spirit),[1] the phrase "filled with the Spirit", πλησθῆναι
πνεύματος (which preserves the conviction that every
manifestation of the Spirit is always an act of God and
proceeds from God).[2] The believer "has" the Spirit in
exactly the same way as, through Jesus Christ, he "has"
a faithful God, in whose continually renewed action he
can put his trust.

3. *The physical manifestations of the Spirit*

In the story of Jesus' baptism, Luke adds that the Spirit
descended "in bodily form" (σωματικῷ εἴδει): and he no
longer means this to be regarded as merely something
which Jesus saw in a vision.[3] He attaches importance
to the objective character of the descent of the Spirit.
It is the same when he is so ready to report the visible
apparitions at Pentecost,[4] or when he takes an earthquake
as evidence for the reality of the event (Acts ii. 3–6; iv. 31).
It is in this connection, too, that prophesying (προφητεύειν)
in times of crisis takes the form of speaking with tongues
(Acts ii. 4; x. 46; xix. 6), a phenomenon astounding
enough to convince even those who are not yet involved.

Luke is a Hellenist. This means, among other things,
that he can only conceive of power in the form of a substance (see above p. 18, n. 2). Nevertheless his real
interest is elsewhere. Unlike a Hellenist he never describes *how* the Spirit impinges upon men. Thus al-

[1] Acts vi. 3; xi. 24; cf. vii. 55; Luke iv. 1. It is also presupposed in Acts
ii. 38; xix. 2; Luke ii. 25. Cf. also the imperf. ἐπληροῦντο Acts xiii. 52.

[2] For the individual, Acts iv. 8; xiii. 9; for the Church, iv. 31. This
passage is too thin to be an old variation on the Pentecost story, and iv. 8
would then be impossible. See further Luke i. 41, 67 and i. 15; Acts ii. 4;
ix. 17, where it is thought of as a permanent possession.

[3] Matthew had already avoided this by saying that the "heavens
opened".

[4] It is not quite certain whether the flames were thought of as perceptible
to everyone, though the noise certainly was. Nevertheless the Spirit is not
identified with the dove or with the fire and wind (ὡς, ὥσπερ, ὡσεί).

though he takes for granted the concept of Spirit as a substance, this is not his real concern.   What concerns him is that the manifestations of the Spirit are visible and ascertainable.   Accordingly it is precisely these manifestations which are important to him, indeed more important than to the other New Testament witnesses.[1]   The Spirit sends those unambiguous pointers from God which admit of no contradiction.[2]

Many of these statements doubtless need to be corrected in the light of other New Testament passages; but the important thing is the conception of the Spirit making man's corporal nature subject to God.   Such is the extent of its activity.

4. *The working of the Spirit*

The sin against the Spirit is unpardonable; but according to Luke xii. 10 (see above p. 37) the Spirit as the power of God no longer manifests itself in casting out demons,[3] but (as xii. 12 makes clear) in the inspired speech of those who witness to Jesus.[4]   Thus Luke is taking over the typically Jewish conception of the Spirit as the Spirit of prophecy (see above p. 7).   Another indication of this is Luke iv. 23–27, where it is in fact denied that the miracles named in iv. 18 are manifestations of the Spirit, and the fulfilment of the prophecy is seen only in the authority of

---

[1] Acts x. 47; xi. 17; xv. 8.   Yet for all that he does not forget that for those who have not faith none of these manifestations is unambiguous, Acts ii. 13.

[2] It is true that, strictly speaking, xxi. 4 asserts that the Spirit can also give a false direction.   Thus here too man's responsible decision is not dispensed with.   Yet in fact Luke is only emphasizing the correctness of the Spirit's prophecy: it was the advice with which it was combined which was false (though humanly understandable).

[3] This tends to fade out in Acts (Jackson-Lake, I, v. 108).

[4] So Lampe, *op. cit.* 190–1.   The only question is whether the disciples are being encouraged (in which case it is their persecutors who commit the sin) or warned (in which case it is themselves, when they do not heed the voice of the Spirit, and fail to confess).   Two reasons make the second alternative preferable: (i) the similarly phrased saying in xii. 8–9 is certainly addressed to the disciples; (ii) in Acts xxvi. 11, where the context is the same, βλασφημεῖν refers to the disciples.   Luke xii. 10 raises the previous two verses to a higher key.

the new preaching.[1]   Although the miracles are of the
greatest importance for Luke, they are never once ascribed
to the Spirit.   What brings salvation is the name of Jesus,
faith in Jesus, Jesus himself, prayer, physical contact with
the disciples, a shadow or a handkerchief[2]—in other
words, the power ($\delta\acute{v}\nu\alpha\mu\iota\varsigma$) of Jesus.[3]   And although
Luke is able to use power ($\delta\acute{v}\nu\alpha\mu\iota\varsigma$) and Spirit ($\pi\nu\epsilon\hat{v}\mu\alpha$)
almost synonymously,[4] in this case the distinction is clear.
Not that Luke does not regard the evidence afforded by
the Spirit as miraculous.   He certainly does so where it is
a case of speaking with tongues,[5] and also in a case where
a momentary inspiration produces a vision of the future.[6]
The same goes for the prophetic insight by which the
apostle, under the influence of the Spirit, sees into the
normally hidden thoughts of another and declares to him
his own heart.[7]   The activity of the Spirit which is
emphasized most strongly is the apprehension of God's
otherwise mysterious will, and this in such a way that it
provides direct instructions for concrete action.[8]

However, the chief thing for which the Spirit is res-

[1] Unlike Matt. xi. 5=Luke vii. 22, though there $\pi\nu\epsilon\hat{v}\mu\alpha$ is not mentioned.

[2] References: Acts iii. 6, 16; iv. 30; v. 15; ix. 34, 40; xvi. 18; xix. 13;
xx. 10; xxviii. 8.   The distinction is particularly clear in iv. 31β, despite
W. Knox, *Acts*, 88).

[3] Luke v. 17; vi. 19 (an addition to the tradition).

[4] Luke xxiv. 49; Acts. i. 5, 8; Luke i. 17; iv. 14—already connected in
Micah iii. 8 (H. A. Guy, *N.T. Prophecy*, 90, A.b.).

[5] Acts ii. 4 (see below, p. 47). x. 46; xix. 6; and also viii. 18.

[6] Luke i. 41, 67; Acts xi. 28; xx. 23; xxi. 4, 11; cf. i. 16; iv. 25; xxviii. 25.
In two borrowed passages, Luke i. 41, 67, it is in a more general way the
disposition of the speaker which is described as controlled by the Spirit,
whereas in Acts it is the utterance itself.   People prophesy $\delta\iota\grave{a}$ $\tau o\hat{v}$ $\pi\nu\epsilon\acute{v}\mu\alpha\tau o\varsigma$,
or else $\pi\nu\epsilon\hat{v}\mu\alpha$ itself is the subject.   Luke x. 21 is original to Luke (see above
p. 38, n. 4); as the other passages show, it is not $\acute{a}\gamma\alpha\lambda\lambda\acute{\iota}\alpha\sigma\iota\varsigma$ as such, but,
only as expressed in prophetic testimony, which is an activity of the Spirit.

[7] Acts xiii. 9.

[8] Acts viii. 29; x. 19; xi. 12; xiii. 2, 4; xvi. 6–7.   xx. 22 is also to be
understood in this way ($\acute{a}\gamma\iota o\nu$ is often omitted in references to the divine
$\pi\nu\epsilon\hat{v}\mu\alpha$), in which case the instruction of the Spirit is made directly to
Paul, whereas xx. 23 refers to instructions given to other brethren.   Presumably the same goes for vii. 51, though vii. 55 is somewhat different,
since here the Spirit makes possible a vision of heaven in the hour of death
—although this too leads to $\mu\alpha\rho\tau\upsilon\rho\epsilon\hat{\iota}\nu$ in word and deed.

ponsible is the preaching of the disciples. This is a wondrous work of God; it takes place in the face of a hostile and persecuting world.[1] That Luke regards prophesying, προφητεύειν, as the central and decisive activity of the Spirit, is shown by his insertion of this word into the long and otherwise almost unaltered quotation from Joel about the eschatological outpouring of the Spirit.[2] For Luke, the Church of the Last Age is a church of prophets. It is only as an afterthought that certain phrases appear in which the Spirit is understood in a general way as abiding in the individual or in the Church.[3]

It is not easy to come to a decision about Acts v. 3, 9. It is very unlikely, at least as far as Luke is concerned, that this is a description of the sin against the Spirit on the lines of Mark iii. 28–9. Moreover the idea can hardly be that the apostles as such are in possession of the Spirit: it is more likely to be the same as in xiii. 9. It is perhaps a prior question, whether xv. 28 (and perhaps xx. 28) does not betray the attitude of a later age, according to which the decision of the Church authority is *eo ipso* the decision of the Holy Spirit. Nevertheless the fact that πνεῦμα and ἡμεῖς crop up side by side, and that there is no mention of anything like πνεῦμα ἐν ἡμῖν makes it probable that Luke, here as elsewhere, means the prophetic Spirit, with which the ἡμεῖς are associated.[4] In this case xx. 28 is also to be explained on the lines of xiii. 1–3; and the important thing to notice is that Luke presupposes the working of the Spirit on all occasions and not just on exceptional ones. Herein lies the possibility of a subsequent misconception, which

[1] Luke xii. 12 is taken from tradition, but given greater emphasis by juxtaposition to xii. 10 (see above, p. 41). Also Acts i. 8; iv. 8, 31; vi. 10; v. 32 is also to be taken in this way: the testimony of the Spirit does not consist in the visible event of Pentecost, but in the preaching of the Apostles and all "those who obey". In Acts xviii. 25 (see below, p. 51), as also in v. 32; vi. 10, a permanent qualification for giving testimony is mentioned; and the power of God referred to in Luke i. 17 and iv. 14 seems to be mainly expressed in the form of proclamation.

[2] Acts ii. 18. D it. read the O.T. text. Cf. Luke ii. 26.

[3] It corresponds to σοφία (Acts vi. 3), πίστις (vi. 5; xi. 24), φόβος τοῦ κυρίου (ix. 31), χαρά (xiii. 52).

[4] Cf. v. 32 and n. 1 above.

automatically associates the Spirit with a correctly per-
formed commission of the Church (see below, p. 108).

One passage is peculiar: Acts viii. 39, where the
catching away of Philip is attributed to the Spirit. One
cannot get round the miraculous element simply by
taking the (dubious) reading ἀπ' αὐτοῦ into the text.[1]
In any case there are numerous parallels to a miraculous
snatching away (I Kings xviii. 12; II Kings ii. 16; Ezek.
iii. 14; viii. 3; Ev. Hebr. (Orig. *Comm. in Joh.* II, 12); Bel
and the Dragon 36; Herm. v. I, i. 3; II. i. 1; Philostr. *Vit.
Ap.* VIII, 10—in Rome in the morning, at Puteoli in the
afternoon). On the other hand, it is possible that the A
reading is original, which attributes the snatching to the
angel. The peculiarity of the Spirit-concept in the usual
text and the regularity with which otherwise, right up to
chapter x, the outpouring of the Spirit is reported or at
least promised, is an argument for this. The omission
could have arisen either from a mechanical slip from
πνεῦμα to κυρίου or from dogmatic considerations (there
is no apostle here to pass on the Spirit). Otherwise it
must be a passage left over from pre-Lucan tradition.

In short, Luke shares with Judaism the concept of
spirit as essentially prophetic Spirit.[2] This prevents him
from regarding the Spirit as the direct source of gifts
of healing, χαρίσματα ἰαμάτων,[3] on the one hand, and
on the other hand of more distinctly ethical phenomena
such as the community life of the early Church.[4] Luke
is still fairly close to the way of thinking which measures
the work of the Spirit by its extraordinariness. Nevertheless it is not the extraordinariness of it as such which
concerns him so much as the fact that God gives to his
Church clear directions and visible signs of his activity.
Preaching, a gift of the Spirit, is certainly always conceived of as a miracle, but not usually as something extra-

[1] Th. Zahn, *Apostelgeschichte, ad loc.*

[2] Guy, *op. cit.* 93, A.a. Lampe, *op. cit.*, 193.

[3] I Cor. xii. 28. Similarly in the O.T. miracles are not ascribed directly
to the רוח, but only to the possessor of the Spirit.

[4] L. S. Thornton, *The Common Life in the Body of Christ*, 6, 74–5, and
C. H. Dodd, *The Apostolic Preaching*, 137, overlook the fact that this is not
actually stated to be due to the Spirit. For Luke, it is not moral renewal
but missionary enterprise which is the gift of the Spirit.

ordinary[1]; for it is particularly in preaching that the activity of the Spirit is bestowed on the Church. However strongly Luke the Hellenist is interested in the *visible* activity of the Spirit, the limitation of this to prophetic preaching remains thoroughly Jewish.[2]

5. *The Spirit as a characteristic of the Age of the Church*

In Luke xi. 13, those who pray to God are promised the πνεῦμα ἅγιον, the Holy Spirit. Originally the promise was simply of "good things" ἀγαθά (Matt. vii. 11)[3]. This correction on Luke's part is understandable in so far as he regards ἀγαθά as worldly goods and therefore suspect; but it also indicates that for him the Spirit is quite simply the gift which is given to the faithful in Jesus' Church.[4] Mark and Matthew saw the Spirit as an eschatological event. But loyalty to the Old Testament view that the Spirit's appearance was something out of the ordinary was still so strong that apart from the Baptism formula only *one* Church *Logion* invoked the momentary aid of the Spirit in particular cases of need. But Luke knows that the Old Testament prophecies promising the Spirit to the people of the Last Age (Num. xi. 29, see above p. 12) are fulfilled. And this means that the Spirit

[1] In the second half of Acts, where fewer sources are drawn on, there is in general less of the miraculous element, in the sense of the extraordinary, and direct injunctions of the Spirit take the place of those given through angels in the first part (Knox, *op. cit.* 91–2; Acts xxvii. 23 is a dream). Even in iv. 31 the Church prays for παρρησία, not γλωσσολαλία. In Acts ix. 27–8 παρρησία is *proof* of the genuineness of Paul's conversion, a reference to which forms the conclusion to Acts (xxviii. 31).

[2] Luke's lack of interest in the process by which the spiritual substance penetrates a man (cf. Verbeke, *op. cit.* 396–7) sets him apart from the Hellenistic conception of πνεῦμα μαντικόν. This is the only mode in which it is true that Acts "represents the power of the Spirit of Jesus assuming historical form in the apostles" (Harnack).

[3] πνεῦμα ἅγιον is a Lucan expression, which he is apt to introduce in other places.

[4] This would receive still greater emphasis if the prayer, "may thy holy Spirit come upon us and cleanse us" (Luke xi. 2), is the oldest reading (Klostermann, *Lukas, ad loc.*; Lampe, *op. cit.* 184; R. Leaney, *The Lucan text of the Lord's Prayer*, Nov. Test. 1 (1956), 103–11).

is given to all members of the Church, and given to them
for ever.

Thus it is presupposed in Acts xix. 2 that everyone who
is baptized possesses the Spirit, and moreover possesses it
visibly and tangibly. The same goes for ii. 38–9, where
the promise of the Spirit is explicitly extended to everyone; also for xv. 8–9, where in particular the Gentiles are
included; and for those passages (viii. 16–18, 39 (see
above); ix. 17; x. 44; xi. 16–17; xix. 6) which see the gift
of the Spirit as the natural consequence of accepting the
faith.[1]

In Luke's account of the outpouring of the Spirit one
is at first inclined to see the decisive eschatological event.
At any rate, the quotation from Joel describes it as such
(Acts ii. 17–21),[2] and indeed there is an eschatological
colouring to the description of the happenings at Pentecost. The one common language is a phenomenon of
the Last Age.[3] Nevertheless, despite ἤκουον in ii. 6 and
ἀκούομεν in ii. 8, the author is not dealing simply with
something miraculously heard.

> The analysis of the section is very difficult. It is
> historically probable that there was some decisive experi-
> ence in the original Church of an outpouring of the Spirit,
> and this may possibly have been the first appearance of
> speaking with tongues.[4] But the question is, how this
> came to be understood as a linguistic miracle. It is
> impossible to explain the story by reference to the Greek
> custom of calling on the Godhead πάσῃ φωνῇ καὶ πάσῃ

[1] From xi. 19 onwards there are no references to a pouring out of the
Spirit except in xix. 6. But this only means that Luke takes from the
tradition reports of objectively authenticated gifts of the Spirit, and sees in
them a particular instance of God's guidance at moments of crisis.

[2] The addition of ἐν ταῖς ἐσχάταις ἡμέραις (ii. 17) stamps the pouring
out of the Spirit as an eschatological event, though this may be a later
correction.

[3] Test. Jud. xxv. 3; Plut. *Is. et Os.* 47 (II, 370b); cf. Isa. lxvi. 18–19.
Paul also takes Isa. xxviii. 11 as referring to γλωσσολαλία, and so earmarks it
as a phenomenon of the Last Age (I Cor. xiv. 21).

[4] Only as regards ii. 13. The misunderstanding, which is then answered
by an apostle, is an invention by Luke in his usual style (Acts iii. 11–12; xiv.
11–15; cf. iv. 9–10; vi. 13–14; xvii. 22–3). Elsewhere in Acts, speaking
with tongues accompanies moments of decisive progress.

διαλέκτῳ. Again the suggestion that Luke simply mis-
understood γλῶσσα since he no longer had any knowledge
of speaking with tongues, is incompatible with x. 46 and
xix. 6. Nevertheless, it could be Luke who was responsible for the details of the story. He understood the
first gift of the Spirit as something *sui generis* and so he could
place an event of this kind at the beginning of Acts just as
he placed Luke iv. 16–30 at the beginning of his gospel.[1]

However, it is far more likely that well before Luke's
time the concept of the New Covenant, of the renewal of
the Law for Judaism all over the world,[2] powerfully
moulded the story of the Spirit's first appearance. There
is no doubt that Jub. vi. 17, 19 is anyhow pre-Christian,
as is Philo's description of the divine voice on Sinai,
which produces a particular echo in each individual soul,
turns itself into a flame, and passes like a πνεῦμα through
a trumpet, so that it is heard by the nearest and the
farthest and reaches to the end of the earth (*Decal.* 33,
35; *Spec. Leg.* II, 189).[3] If by A.D. 70 Pentecost was
already observed as the conclusion of the Passover which
celebrates the release from Egypt, and if the day of
the gift of the Law (Deut. iv. 10; ix. 10; xviii. 16 LXX)
was already referred to as ἡ ἡμέρα τῆς ἐκκλησίας, this
kind of interpretation would have been a natural one.
It is likely that in the (unorthodox) circles of Jubilees and
perhaps also among the sects, Pentecost was celebrated as
the "Oath Festival", on which the covenant was renewed
and the spiritual year began. The Baptist's saying about
one who would baptize with storm and fire[4] could have
been turned into history, and so could have determined
the formulation of Acts ii, 2–3. Luke takes over the
story, not attaching much importance to it (unlike
Matthew) as a statement of the new Law,[5] but regarding
it as the beginning of the period of the Church and at the
same time as a precursor of the progress of the Gospel
among the nations. This presumably leads him to think

---

[1] Lampe, *op. cit.* 159.

[2] Knox, *op. cit.* 80–2. On the list of the peoples, *ibid.* 84, n. 1. The
eschatological reunion of all the dispersed was a living hope.

[3] Law and Fire are also combined in Rabbinic literature (Str.-B. II,
603–4).

[4] See above, pp. 28–9.

[5] Luke no longer makes the Sermon on the Mount correspond to the
Sinai proclamation, as Matthew does (so Knox, *op. cit.* 81–2, rightly).
But this is not because Pentecost takes its place.

of the language of the Spirit as a new miracle language understood by all; and maybe the idea of an antitype to the Babel story in Gen. xi. played its part also.[1]

Yet this episode, for Luke, is not the decisive eschatological one. It introduces a new age, but not *the* new age. Between the O.T. salvation-narrative and the history of the mission, he makes the Christ-event "the mid-point of time".[2] Consequently it is possible for the outpouring of the Spirit to be repeated whenever men are drawn to the faith. It takes on special forms, when a new step is taken into the world of the Gentiles (Acts viii. 17–18; x. 44 ff.). That the beginning of Luke's gospel allows for men being filled with the Spirit shows only that this was drawn from tradition,[3] and was regarded by Luke as a presage of what was to come. On the other hand, Luke occasionally avoids the expression that an O.T. writer speaks "in the spirit". (Contrast Mark xii. 36 with Luke xx. 42; but cf. Acts i. 16; xxviii. 25.) The same goes for the corresponding concept of δύναμις at the Parousia (Mark ix. 1).

Luke has gone ahead of Mark and Matthew by an important step. He is not content with occasional spiritual traits or even with the nativity and baptism narratives for portraying Jesus as the bearer of the Spirit. His real concern is with the age of the Church. This is where the prophecies about the People of God are fulfilled; for it is to this people in its totality that the Spirit is given. Prophets no longer come by ones and twos. All the members of the ultimate Church are prophets.

---

[1] J. G. Davies, *Pentecost and Glossolalia*, J.T.S. N.S.3 (1952), 228–9.

[2] Cf. G. Vos, *The Eschatological Aspect of the Pauline conception of the Spirit*, Biblical and Theological Studies, Princeton (1912), 223–4. Yet the differences from Paul, in view of Rom. ix–xi, must not be exaggerated. For Luke, too, nothing more can happen in history greater than the salvation wrought by Christ. History, in fact, is now the history of faith in that salvation, i.e. the history of the mission.

[3] Goguel, *Notion*, 45, n. 1. Lampe, *op. cit.* 167, thinks differently. This is indicated by the strong connection with temple worship of all those who are endowed with the Spirit (except Mary). It is consequently very unlikely that Luke consciously composed this prelude under the influence of Joel iii. 1–2 (Guy, *op. cit.* 28–9).

The limitations of his vision and his indebtedness to Jewish tradition become apparent here. Basically, he cannot get away from understanding the Spirit only as an exceptional power which makes possible unusual feats of strength. It is true that this conception was counteracted by two things; first by the Jewish tradition, which almost confined the Spirit to the activity of inspiring prophetic utterance; secondly, by what was now an article of faith, that all members of the new Church possess the Spirit. This implied that the Spirit could not be present *only* in paranormal manifestations. Nevertheless Luke remained true to the old conception. Granted that the Spirit must have ways of showing itself which are not outwardly abnormal, for instance, in παρρησία (see above, p. 45 n. 1), nevertheless it does not automatically launch the believer on a completely new "eschatological" way of life; it simply imparts to him a special gift to equip him for quite definite additional expressions of his faith, things which are essential for the still incomplete, still expanding history of the mission—things indeed which alone make the mission possible.

There is also a negative side to this: faith is never derived from the Spirit, even in places where Luke goes out of his way to underline the fact that "believing", πιστεῦσαι, is not a natural phenomenon, but something which is miraculously given by God.[1] Even the ideal condition of the Church can be described without any mention of the Spirit,[2] nor is salvation ever based upon it.[3] According to Acts ii. 38, those who repent and are baptized receive the Spirit; but v. 32 adds, that obedience is a condition of receiving it. Days, or in exceptional cases even weeks or years, can elapse before the gift of the Spirit follows faith, though this does not mean that the believer returns to the

---

[1] Acts xvi. 14: ὁ κύριος διήνοιξεν τὴν καρδίαν; iii. 16: ἡ πιστις ἡ δι' αὐτοῦ (=Jesus).

[2] E.g. Acts ii. 42–7.

[3] This is an entirely Jewish attitude. In Hellenism salvation comes by apotheosis and rebirth, Jackson-Lake, I, i. 326.

status of a non-believer (ix. 17: viii. 16; xix. 2). In the same way prayer is never understood as an act of the Spirit, but as a preparation for receiving it (see below p. 52 n. 3).

Thus it would certainly not be correct to connect only "extraordinary" religious activity with the Spirit;[1] nevertheless in Luke the Spirit only gives the power necessary to fulfil a particular task, or to express faith in some concrete action. Therefore the difference between this concept of the Spirit and the Old Testament attitude consists only in that in the new Age of Salvation not only the individual but the whole Church is a bearer of the Spirit, and that, as a result of the recent development of the Spirit-concept in Judaism, the operation of the Spirit is almost entirely understood in connection with prophecy.

In other words, the peculiarity of Luke's testimony lies in its demonstration that a church which has no special power to fulfil its missionary task in a concrete way is a church without the Spirit. By not yet ascribing to the Spirit the very existence of the Church, Luke reminds the Church how necessary is that activity which is the gift of the Spirit.

6. *How the Spirit is received*

Normally the Spirit is given by baptism in the Name of Jesus. The reason why the disciples in Acts xix. 2 have not received the Spirit is presumably that they have not been baptized. In ix. 17 Paul is promised the gift of the Spirit, and this seems to be automatically fulfilled by the baptism in the next verse. In ii. 38, baptism at any rate precedes endowment with the Spirit. But in x. 44–48 it is the other way round. The pouring out of the Spirit precedes baptism, although it still does not make baptism unnecessary.

---

[1] Thus (a) παρρησία is derived from the Spirit, even when it has no abnormal form; (b) miracles of healing are not.

It is questionable how far these passages are based on correct historical recollection. In xi. 15–17 baptism is not mentioned at all. Instead of κωλῦσαι τὸ ὕδωρ (x. 47) appears κωλῦσαι τὸν θεόν. The quotation in xi. 16β only makes sense so long as no baptism by water follows, or at least so long as it remains unimportant. According to xi. 3, Peter is only accused of sharing table-fellowship, not baptism; yet it cannot be inferred from this that the baptism in x. 44–8 is a later addition. If Luke had added this here, why not also in xi. 3 and 17? On the contrary it must be inferred that in x. 47–8 he took over from tradition the reference to baptism without attaching any great importance to it. For xi. 6, as i. 5 shows, is certainly a Lucan addition, and proves that Luke thought of baptism as at most incidental to the all-important outpouring of the Spirit.

Further, the precise meaning of ii. 38 is that for Luke baptism is simply a natural episode in what he regards as much more important, namely conversion.[1] Consequently he does not pause to consider that, a moment before, the Spirit had been poured out on the 120 (I. 15) without baptism—which proves that he did not regard baptism as essential for acquiring the Spirit. The same goes for xix. 1–7, especially if one considers it along with xviii. 25. xix. 1–7, according to Luke, is about Christians who have had no experience of the Holy Spirit. It is historically possible that twelve disciples of John were converted by Paul, so that in the earliest narrative the baptism of John, which involves no gift of the Spirit, was distinguished from the baptism of Jesus, which does.[2] Similarly, Luke regards Apollos as being already a Christian, whereas historically he was probably a Jewish missionary who again was first converted in Ephesus. In the one case a baptism was in the tradition, in another case not. In Luke's account there is no room either for a Jewish missionary working "in the spirit" or for a group that has remained loyal to the Baptist. Both stories serve him as illustrations of the progress of salvation

---

[1] In Qumran, *Manual of Discipline*, iii. 4–12; v. 13, baptism is an outward sign of the conversion which has already happened, and which alone purifies.

[2] The passage certainly does not prove that the Baptist said nothing about the Spirit, but only that those disciples had not experienced the actual outpouring of it. Cf. B. W. Bacon in *The Expositor*, VI, 10 (1904), 14.

from the O.T., through the Baptist, to the Church. But we cannot infer from this that there was a time when spirit-baptism made water-baptism seem unnecessary.[1] It is unlikely that even at the beginning baptism could have had merely a negative significance as a cleansing rite and been disconnected from the pouring out of the Spirit.[2] At the very least baptism was always a necessary condition for receiving the Spirit.

It looks then, as if Luke either takes over from tradition the connection between baptism and reception of the Spirit, or else uses the word baptism as a natural expression for conversion, without laying any special emphasis upon it. As a preparation for receiving the Spirit, Luke regards prayers as far more important than baptism,[3] and as a condition for it, he always mentions faith ($\pi\iota\sigma\tau\epsilon\hat{\upsilon}\sigma\alpha\iota$ ii. 38, viii. 12; ix. 1–19, etc.) According to xv. 8–9 it is faith, not baptism, which cleanses one for receiving the Spirit. Nevertheless, Luke does not regard water-baptism as an unnecessary external rite. He is no "spiritualist" who knows only of spirit-baptism.[4] What is more imporant is that in Acts it is the freedom of the Spirit which is most strongly emphasized. The Spirit does not limit itself to baptism. At one time it falls upon men before their baptism (x. 44), at another time without any baptism at all (ii. 1–4) and once (xviii. 25) upon a disciple who only knows of the baptism of John which, according to xix. 3–4, is unable to confer the Spirit on others.[5]

But is there not evidence in viii. 14–17 that the gift of the Spirit is dependent upon a laying on of hands by the

[1] Flemington, op. cit. 44, n. 1; 45. Contrast Jackson-Lake, I, i. 337–43. On the historical question of the appearance of Baptism see Kraeling, op. cit. 171–5.

[2] On the other side see Bultmann, T.N.T. I, 139.

[3] Luke iii. 21; Acts ix. 9, 11 for the first, and Acts iv. 31; xiii. 1–3 for a repeated reception of the Spirit. In viii. 15 the Apostles pray for it, and in viii. 18–20 a misunderstanding in terms of magic is sharply repudiated.

[4] Otherwise he could neither write ii. 38 nor incorporate x. 47–8; xix. 5.

[5] On the freedom of the Spirit cf. also x. 20 (where ἐγώ is emphasized); xiii. 1–4; xvi. 6–7; xx. 22–3; xxi. 4, 11.

apostles? Is not this passage at least an early instance of
"Catholicism", where the Spirit appears to be dependent
on order and ritual, and no longer the other way round?
Hardly, for this passage is peculiar. In ii. 38 and x. 48,
no laying on of hands is mentioned.[1] In ix. 12 the action
is taken by an ordinary member of the Church, and although laying on of hands is mentioned, it is only in order
to heal![2] No, Luke's main interest is in the free working
of the Spirit, even in passages where in fact the decisive
issues are ones of "ecclesiastical politics". He knows, for
instance, about the collection for Jerusalem (Acts xxiv.
17), which Paul himself regarded as a kind of token of
loyalty towards Jerusalem, rather like the Jewish Temple
tax. (Gal. ii. 10; Rom. xv. 27). But Luke does not describe this in any way as an expression of an integrated
ecclesiastical organization, but prefers to give an account
of it which derives such a collection from free prophetic
inspiration (xi. 28). Again, in viii. 14–17, it does not
seem to be the ritual laying on of hands or the authority
of the apostles which is important, but only the connection
with Jerusalem. Just as the beginning of Luke's gospel
is linked to Jewish piety, so Acts viii. 14–17 is evidence that
the Spirit does not lead the Church at one leap into completely new territory, but that its activity is closely related
to the history which preceded it. That is why not only
apostles have to "come down from Jerusalem" (viii. 14–
15), but also prophets who speak from the occasional
inspiration of the Spirit (xi. 27). That is why, again,
Paul's journey to Jerusalem is so strongly emphasized, just
as Jesus' is in the gospel. The movement of God's
history is from Jerusalem outwards and then always back

---

[1] Even if this were because it was taken for granted and therefore not
mentioned (Flemington, *op. cit.* 44, n. 1—is that why it is never mentioned
in Paul at all?), it would still not be essential for Luke. The same goes
for Luke xix. 6, where the whole *pericope* shows that it is not the laying on of
the apostles' hands which matters, but Jesus' baptism.

[2] And this is not because only an apostle could pass on the Spirit: for in
ix. 17 it is expected that it will be passed on *by* Ananias. In xiii. 3, too, it
is not the apostles who lay on hands. Cf. also viii. 39 (A text).

again.   Later on, the idea develops into something like
a caliphate at Jerusalem; but for Luke it only goes to con-
firm the progress of God's work of redemption.

Appendix: miscellaneous usages of πνεῦμα

In Luke i. 47, 80, πνεῦμα appears in a psychological
sense; nevertheless in both passages it seems that there is
still a strong echo of the concept of God's power standing
apart from a man and being only temporarily imparted
to him (see above, p. 38 n.1).   Acts xvii. 16 is to be understood as equivalent to Luke i. 47, whereas in Acts xix. 21,
as in Luke ii. 27, the reference is to the Spirit of God; so
also in Acts xviii. 25; xx. 22 (see above, p. 51).   πνεῦμα
appears (a) as that part of a man which survives death[1] in
Luke viii. 55 (which is new compared with Mark), (b)
in a quotation in Luke xxiii. 46, and (c) in a passage
dependent on this, Acts vii. 59.   It is questionable
whether one can conclude from Luke xxiii. 43, Acts ii. 24,
31–2, that Luke thought of Jesus existing during the
triduum mortis in the form of πνεῦμα as distinct from the
(incorruptible) σάρξ.[2]   Luke xxiv. 37, 39; Acts xxiii. 8–9
are anyhow completely unhellenistic in that πνεῦμα
means a ghostly, bodily existence which is precisely the
opposite of ἐγὼ αὐτός (Luke xxiv. 39).

c. PAUL

1. *Old Testament and Hellenistic antecedents*[3]

All that has been discussed so far has taken its basic
character from the Old Testament.   As in the Old Testament and as throughout Judaism, the Spirit has appeared,
not as a necessary condition of salvation, but as the power
required for special feats.   Granted this conception, it was

---

[1] Jub. xxiii. 26–31; Eth. Enoch xxii; xxxix. 4 ff. etc.

[2] Cf. the disembodied souls of the blessed in Lucian *Verae Historiae*, II,
12.

[3] On the one hand, in Judaism (and still more in the development of
Christendom) Hellenistic and Palestinian communities exercised a powerful
influence on each other; and on the other hand, Gnosticism seems insepar-
able from a heterodox Judaism which was under the influence of Iranian
and Hellenistic dualism.   In Paul, too, it is hard to distinguish between
the two.

hardly possible that the Spirit could appear as anything but
a sign of some still imminent reality.   In the quotation
from Joel (Acts ii. 19–21) the pouring out of the Spirit is
still clearly represented as the beginning of the cata-
clysm of the Last Age, and in Hebrews vi. 4–5 the Spirit
which works miracles is a foretaste of the good things of
the world to come.   But this is to make the Spirit no more
than a somewhat irregular prelude to the Parousia, a wel-
come but basically inessential presage of the impending
reality.   After all, the existence of all kinds of new miraculous powers does not amount to an assurance of one's
own salvation.

Luke could attempt to get over this, since he lived at a
time when there was no longer a lively expectation of the
Parousia.   But this is precisely where the dilemma arose.
The Parousia was displaced by the mission period.
Therefore the Spirit could no longer be a warrant of
eschatological salvation; it must be a power working
through the history of the intervening period.   Yet,
despite all the different interpretations, the main question
remained.   How was the proclamation of the Spirit
connected with that of the crucified, risen and coming
Lord?[1]

When the witness of Christianity spread to men who
were influenced by Greek thought, it was transplanted into
a community unfamiliar with the concept of a progressive
and purposeful history.[2]   Such people were not accus-
tomed to the old idea of one age succeeding another: if
they were dualists at all, they thought in terms of opposing
spheres.[3]   Therefore they certainly could not conceive of
the Spirit as a mere *sign* of that which is to come.   If it
were part of the heavenly world, it must be the reality
itself.   Now the Hellenist always thought of power as a
material substance;[1] therefore for him the coming of the

[1] This is the decisive question for primitive Christianity.
[2] O. Cullmann, *Christ and Time*, E.T. 51–58. Gnosticism is a "révolte
contre le temps", G. Quispel in Eranos Jbch. 16 (1948), 122, n. 23.
[3] For the Gnostic view, see above, p. 19.

Spirit could only mean the irruption of celestial matter. If Jesus were the bringer of the Spirit, he must have been a bearer of celestial matter, with which he endowed believers and so united them with the celestial world. Thus, for the first time, a radical solution became possible. The meaning of Jesus' mission lay in his bringing the celestial power-substance, $\pi\nu\epsilon\hat{\upsilon}\mu\alpha$, into the world. Union with him meant union with this substance, that is to say with heaven, that is to say, salvation itself.

We can still see in second-century Gnosticism (where this possibility was taken to its logical conclusion) how this interpretation must have looked in its early stages. The meaning of Jesus' whole mission lay entirely in his bestowal of the Spirit; and the Spirit meant salvation—though at the same time it meant the nature, $\phi\acute{\upsilon}\sigma\iota\varsigma$, which saves the "spiritual" man.[2]

It followed inevitably from this last point that the "spiritual" nature of man should be thought of as having existed all along. In that case the act of redemption could not create any change in him, but could only help him to understand it.[3] Did it not follow that all that was necessary to give him this understanding was a myth? Was it not completely unimportant whether anything had actually happened or not? It is no accident that the Cross had no place in this system, nor that the entire Incarnation could be understood as a piece of deception played on the hostile powers.[4]

In Paul, eschatology is critical. More clearly than all his predecessors, he understood the cross and resurrection,

---

[1] See above, p. 18 n. 2. This Hellenistic substance-concept was of course indebted to primitive concepts which occur just as much in the O.T. as anywhere else (cf. W. D. Davies, *Paul and Rabbinic Judaism*, 184, for Rabbinic examples); but only in Hellenism did it become normative for theory about the spirit.

[2] See above, p. 21, and (for $\phi\acute{\upsilon}\sigma\epsilon\iota\ \sigma\omega\zeta\acute{o}\mu\epsilon\nu o\varsigma$), p. 22 n. 6.

[3] It is agreed that the Gnostic's knowledge is an understanding of himself. But does not this show precisely that this is *all* it is, and that man *only* meets himself in it?

[4] Lietzmann, *Komm.* ad I Cor. ii. 6 (Exk.).

not as an overture to the Parousia, but as the great turning point in time; life in the Spirit meant life in the new κτίσις, the new created order.[1] In this way he was able to take the Hellenistic interpretation of the Christ-event a stage further. The presence of the Spirit was already clearly connected with the descent and ascent of the Redeemer; it was now no longer just an additional phenomenon, but was manifest in the new existence of the Church itself.

It is clear from Rom. i. 3-4 that "Spirit" (πνεῦμα) was already used to describe the celestial sphere or the celestial substance, and that Paul, for his part, took over this conception.

> The related formula in I Tim. iii. 16 is constructed in rigidly chiastic pairs: a–b/b–a/a–b. σάρξ, ἔθνη, κόσμος correspond to πνεῦμα, ἄγγελοι, δόξα.[2] It follows that ἐν πνεύματι, which is contrasted with ἐν σαρκί, must be rendered "in the sphere of the Spirit". Salvation consists in the new-found unity of the two spheres.[3] πνεῦμα then not merely describes a spatial realm, but qualifies this as the realm of celestial substance. It is taken for granted in all this that the nature of the Redeemer is "spiritual"—that is why the μυστήριον begins with the φανερωθῆναι ἐν σαρκί. The same goes for the phraseology in I Pet. iii. 18β. It would be easy to understand πνεύματι as an instrumental dative,[4] but this is out of the question for σαρκί. Therefore the interpretation here, as in I Tim. iii. 16, must be: in the corporal sphere, in the spiritual sphere.[5]

It is stated in the same passage (Rom. i. 3-4) that Jesus Christ in his corporal existence is the Son of David, in his spiritual existence the Son of God in power. Originally

---

[1] It is to the lasting credit of A. Schweitzer (*Mysticism of Paul the Apostle*, E.T., 160–76), that he pointed this out.

[2] δόξα, like πνεῦμα (cf. I Cor. xv. 43-4; δόξα = δύναμις = πνευματικόν), means the nature of God and also of the angels.

[3] Dibelius, *Pastoralbriefen*[3], *ad loc.* Cf. Kittel, art. *Righteousness*, E.T. 60.

[4] As Calvin did, *In N.T. Commentarii* (ed. Tholuck, 1838), *ad loc.* For the meaning, cf. I. Cor. xv. 45; II Cor. iii. 6; Rom. viii. 11; Ezek. xxxvii.

[5] E. G. Selwyn, *The First Epistle of St. Peter*, 325, draws a parallel between the individual details of the confessions of faith in I Tim. iii. 16 and I Pet. iii. 18–22.

the formula expressed a Christology which made Jesus the Son of God only as a result of his ascension (Acts xiii. 33; ii. 36; cf. the subject of Mark ix. 3, 7). The Church put this schematically in the flesh/spirit contrast (κατὰ σάρκα/κατὰ πνεῦμα) and combined it with the view taken from official Judaism that Jesus was the earthly descendant of David. Paul improves on this by prefixing υἱοῦ αὐτοῦ to the whole formula.

Paul was not the first to use πνεῦμα to mean the sphere of divine glory, which the Redeemer enters when he is exalted.[1] The O.T. contrast between the holy Spirit of God and weak and sinful flesh (Isa. xxxi. 3) begins to take on Hellenistic traits, for which the ground was certainly prepared by the Apocalyptic and Rabbinic distinction between a "lower" and an "upper" world. While for the Jew the characteristic feature of this world is rebellion against God, or at least its transitoriness, for the Hellenist it is its material alienation from God.[2] Human existence is determined by the sphere, the magnetic field, as it were, into which it is inserted.[3] But if the sphere really determines existence, then entry into the spiritual sphere means entry into spiritual existence. Now Christ has entered this, therefore he is necessarily termed πνεῦμα, which is theoretically a statement about his material being, but is in fact a statement about his power, that is, his significance for the Church.

Paul accepts the Gnostic conception of the spirit-body of the ascended κύριος embracing all its members; for his unquestioning use of the phrase σῶμα Χριστοῦ (and also ἐν Χριστῷ) does not introduce this idea so much as presuppose it.[4] The same conception lies behind I Cor. xii. 13. That ἐν σῶμα is identified from the start with ὁ Χριστός in xii. 12 shows that in 13 it cannot mean just the objective which is achieved when all the limbs are

[1] Cf. Phil. ii. 9–11; Rev. v.

[2] I Tim. iii. 16 is probably closer to this, while Rom. i. 3–4 is far more Jewish in feeling.

[3] For a modern statement of this, see C. Michalson, *The Holy Spirit and the Church*, Theology Today, 8 (1951–2), 43–4.

[4] Yet it is quite possible that O.T. conceptions, and the thought of the Body which was sacrificed for us on the cross, also play their part. Cf. E. Schweizer, *Lordship and Discipleship* (S.C.M. Press, 1960), ch. 4.

organically united, but rather the already existing Body into which the believers are baptized.[1] This brings the various concepts together; they describe the spirit element with which the believers are united and with which they are given to drink (13β).[2] In 13α ἐν πνεύματι is probably to be taken instrumentally,[3] as in I Cor. vi. 11. But the power which makes membership possible is no less materially conceived, and corresponds to the frequent phrase ἐν ὕδατι.[4]

So far the relationship between Spirit (πνεῦμα) and the Body of Christ (σῶμα Χριστοῦ) is not yet made clear, but in II Cor. iii. 17 the Lord (κύριος) is identified with Spirit (πνεῦμα).

The interpretation of this passage is of course discutable.[5] The sentence has been taken as an explanatory note to the quotation, pointing out that the κύριος of the quotation means the Spirit (though on the analogy of Gal. iv. 25 we should expect τὸ δὲ κύριος); turning to the *Spirit* would then "lift the veil" and 17 would define this "Spirit" still more precisely as the Spirit of Jesus. The reasons advanced for this view do not hold water. Whatever else the sentence is, it is not a superfluous Christological digression. In iii. 6 and 8 the new service is described and determined not by γράμμα but by the πνεῦμα. It is then shown that unbelieving Judaism still lives under the "veil", which is only removed ἐν Χριστῷ (14). Only turning to the κύριος (=Χριστός 14, as always) can take it away. The statement that this κύριος is the Spirit brings the two series of statements together. Indeed, the identity of the ascended κύριος, to which Israel should return instead of to Moses (cf. Rom. x. 4–5, I Cor. x. 2), with the πνεῦμα, shows that turning to him also means turning to the new διακονία in the πνεῦμα. It cannot be maintained that Paul, even though he readily

[1] Lietzmann, *Kor.*[4] *ad loc.* M. Barth interprets it: "baptized into the body of Christ", *getauft auf den Leib Christi.*
[2] On the image of the out-poured Spirit, cf. Thornton, *op. cit.* 89–91. Water-drinking produces inspiration, Tatian, *Or. Graec.* xix. 3.
[3] Thornton, *op. cit.* 89.
[4] Therefore πνεῦμα can just as well be the causative power of Baptism as the new "element" (13β) which is transmitted through it. Cf. Flemington, *op. cit.* 69; 39, n. 2.
[5] Davies, *op. cit.* 196, n. 1: C. H. Dodd, *History and the Gospel*, 55–7.

ascribes the same functions both to Christ and to the
Spirit, nevertheless never makes the two equivalent (see
below).[1]   It has already been shown (p. 57) that Rom.
i. 4 cannot be adduced as evidence for a second Pauline
conception.

It is clearly stated, then, that the Spirit ($\pi\nu\epsilon\hat{\upsilon}\mu\alpha$) is
the ascended Christ, and that turning unto him is union
with the realm of the Spirit.   Whoever approaches him
enters the sphere of the Spirit.   iii. 17β makes a distinc-
tion between Lord ($\kappa\acute{\upsilon}\rho\iota\sigma$) and Spirit ($\pi\nu\epsilon\hat{\upsilon}\mu\alpha$); but this
is only to clarify 17α, which does not assert the identity
of the two personalities, but only indicates by the word
Spirit the mode in which the Lord exists.   "Spirit of the
Lord" is simply used as a periphrasis for his mode of existence, in other words for the power in which he encounters his Church.[2]   When Christ is seen in terms of his
role for the Church and of his works of power within the
Church, he can be identified with the Spirit; but insofar
as Christ is also Lord over his own power, he can be distinguished from that power, just as "I" can always be
distinguished from the power which goes out of me.   The
same conception is expressed still more precisely in I Cor.
vi. 17; for the basis of this passage is the concept of the
spirit-body of the ascended Lord, which includes believers
within itself.   This organic connection of believers with
Christ is completely analogous to sexual union with a
prostitute; and to underline this, unchastity is reckoned
as a dire sin, precisely because it is consummated *bodily*
and so affects the relationship with Christ.[3]   It is made
explicit in I Cor. xv. 45 that by his resurrection Christ has
become "the spirit that maketh alive" $\pi\nu\epsilon\hat{\upsilon}\mu\alpha$ $\zeta\omega\sigma\pi\sigma\iota\sigma\hat{\upsilon}\nu$.

[1] I Thess. i. 5; II Cor. xii. 9; Phil. iv. 13.   See C. A. A. Scott, *Christianity
according to St. Paul*, 260.   See further II Cor. iv. 10–11 and Col. iii. 4;
Gal. v. 25 and II Cor. iii. 6.

[2] The expression "Spirit of Christ" is very rare in Paul; though cf. Rom.
viii. 9; Phil. i. 19; Gal. iv. 6.

[3] This judgment is traditional (Prov. vi. 23–35; Lietzmann, *Kor.*[4],
ad loc.).

Moreover, on this depends the gift to the believer of a
"spiritual body", σῶμα πνευματικόν.[1] The whole argument depends here upon the presupposition that Christ,
like Adam, embraces the whole of humanity. Paul is
faithful both to the Old Testament patriarch-idea and to
Hellenism; he insists that the resurrection (or ascension) has removed Christ into the sphere of the Spirit,
and that union with him assures the believer of
the same spiritual existence, experienced as life in the
Church.[2]

But Paul was also influenced by early Christian eschatology. For this, the important passage is I Cor. xv,
where Paul's thought starts from the fact of the Resurrection. This is quite unlike the Gnostics, whose only use
for the myth was that it arouses a memory of an already
indwelling reality. For Paul it was a fact, a fact which
had completely altered the situation. It is therefore no
accident that Paul never uses Gnostic language about the
"spiritual substance" of the pre-existent one. But on the
other hand, he has no use for the concept of the "spiritual
body" of the ascended Christ except for explaining to the
Church the significance of Jesus' resurrection for their own
raising from the dead. It is true that in I Cor. xv. 35–50
Paul starts from the Corinthians' own presuppositions.
But he parts company with them precisely in his use
of the phrase "spiritual body", σῶμα πνευματικόν.
They understood it as something which is already given
to the believer and simply survives death; but he sees
it as something given once and for all by God in the
Resurrection. Again, he does not talk about the "living
Spirit", πνεῦμα ζῶν, which would be a kind of con-
tagious life-force, but about the "Spirit which giveth

---

[1] Burton, *Galatians* (I.C.C.), 489; Selwyn, *I Peter*, 282–3, think that this is
the body of the human πνεῦμα, which can do without an earthly body.
This is impossible.

[2] Cf. J. Knox, *Chapters in a Life of Paul*, 128–40; C. H. Dodd, *Romans*
(Moffatt N.T. Commentary), on Rom. vi. 6; J. Moffatt, *I Corinthians* (same
series) on I Cor. xv. 44.

life", πνεῦμα ζωοποιοῦν, that is, about the creative power of the resurrected Lord.[1]

There is no trace here of the idea of a spiritual body underneath the physical body. In fact, Paul actually attacks this idea (xv. 46; 45 merely supports the proposition in 44β; and this is what 46 refers to, not anything in 45, so that the word to be understood is σῶμα). Paul is not warding off an attitude which sought to replace the eschatological coming of the Redeemer by a doctrine of a pre-existent original man: he is fighting a belief in the prime importance of the "spiritual" σῶμα as something belonging by right to man and therefore not first given to him at the Resurrection. 44β, it is true, seems to take it for granted that his opponents have no knowledge of such a thing, but 29 makes it clear that they nevertheless believe in a life after death. Their mistake is that they know of no "spiritual body" in Paul's sense, but only in the Gnostic sense of something hidden beneath the "psychical" body and simply surviving death. That is why in 49 Paul writes φορέσομεν. From the premise that Christ, like Adam, controls all humanity that belongs to him, it is a short step to the Corinthians' conclusion that all who belong to him *are* already ἐπουράνιοι. But for Paul they only "are" so by virtue of their faith in him who will one day make them so, and certainly not by virtue of their physical superiority over the "unspiritual".

There is another view according to which the place of σῶμα in the scheme is merely as the medium through which the change from "fleshly" to "spiritual" substance takes place. But this too is untenable. The particular position taken up by Paul is shown by the contrast between ψυχικός (xv. 44), which is characterized by φθορά (42, 50), ἀσθένεια and ἀτιμία (43, cf. Phil. iii. 21 ταπείνωσις), and πνευματικός characterized by ἀφθαρσία (42, 50) δύναμις and δόξα (43; Phil. iii. 21). Behind this formal thinking in terms of substances lies the O.T. contrast between weakness and strength.[2] Man remains dependent upon the creative power of his Lord, who

[1] A sharper distinction still is made by F. W. Grosheide, *Commentary on I Corinthians* (1953), 387, on I Cor. xv. 45, who thinks that Christ's whole life-work as Mediator, and not just his resurrection, made him πνεῦμα ζωοποιοῦν.

[2] Rom. vi. 19; viii. 26. δόξα is not a material light-flash, as is shown by II Cor. iii. 8–iv. 6.

will resurrect him.[1] The link between earthly and heavenly body is forged by a miracle. The same goes for xv. 47, where "earth" ($\gamma\hat{\eta}$) in the first phrase indicates the stuff of which the "first man" is composed, while the second phrase describes the "second man", not in terms of the substance he is composed of, but in terms of his origin. Consequently the $\sigma\hat{\omega}\mu\alpha$ $\pi\nu\epsilon\upsilon\mu\alpha\tau\iota\kappa\acute{o}\nu$ of the Redeemer, as of the believer, cannot be understood simply as something *composed of* $\pi\nu\epsilon\hat{\upsilon}\mu\alpha$ but as something *controlled by* $\pi\nu\epsilon\hat{\upsilon}\mu\alpha$. Nevertheless, it must not be forgotten that this is only true of Paul's own position. His terminology betrays the fact that, like every Hellenist, he has a material view of power (see above, p. 18 n. 2). Thus, whilst Paul's doctrine is Jewish, his terminology is Hellenistic.

Certain other passages have the same implication:

(*a*) I Cor. vi. 14 starts from the fact of the raising up of Jesus, and emphasizes that the bodily raising up of believers lies in the future.[2] But this leads to another point; the concept of consubstantiality between the believer and Christ, which is apparently expressed by the simile of sexual one-bodyness (see above, p. 60), is not definitive, but is only another way of expressing the connection between two creative acts of God, the raising up of Jesus and the raising up of all believers. $\sigma\hat{\omega}\mu\alpha$, then, cannot here mean just physical substance; indeed it is contrasted with $\kappa\omega\lambda\acute{\iota}\alpha$ which does not qualify for the promise of resurrection (vi. 13). Because $\sigma\hat{\omega}\mu\alpha$ can be replaced by $\hat{\eta}\mu\epsilon\hat{\iota}s$ it is clear that for Paul the important thing about the sexual act is that it is personal. In the same way the association of the believer with Christ, though it is thought of as bodily, is not just physical but personal.

(*b*) In the same way Rom. viii. 11[3] starts from the fact of the resurrection and presupposes that the raising up of believers lies in the future, "because of" the Spirit that dwells in them.[4] Nevertheless there is no suggestion here

---

[1] In this sense even the $\pi\nu\epsilon\upsilon\mu\alpha\tau\iota\kappa\acute{o}s$ belongs to the $\grave{\epsilon}\pi\acute{\iota}\gamma\epsilon\iota o\iota$ (xv. 48–9, 40; E. B. Allo, in Rev. Bib. 43 (1934), 342. The aorist $\grave{\epsilon}\phi o\rho\acute{\epsilon}\sigma\alpha\mu\epsilon\nu$ should be understood in terms of the future $\phi o\rho\acute{\epsilon}\sigma o\mu\epsilon\nu$).

[2] An already accomplished "raising up" of believers is first taught in Col. ii. 12; iii. 1, and even there is qualified by $\delta\iota\grave{\alpha}$ $\pi\acute{\iota}\sigma\tau\epsilon\omega s$.

[3] Cf. Kittel, art. *Sin*, E.T. 83–4.

[4] The accusative (twice in Origen, once in Tertullian) is to be preferred as the *lectio difficilior*, since apart from I Cor. xv. 45 (where it depends on a quotation) $\pi\nu\epsilon\hat{\upsilon}\mu\alpha$ does not mean creative power in Paul.

of a material guarantee,[1] but two ideas are combined: (i) the God who has raised up Jesus is already at work in them through the Spirit, and will continue to so to work after their death; (ii) natural man, as a sinner, is subject to death (viii. 10) but he who is righteous owing to the work of the Spirit (see below, p. 71) will be resurrected (viii. 11).

(c) It is true also of II Cor. iii. 17 that the thought is not dominated by material categories.   This is shown not only by the already mentioned shift to πνεῦμα κυρίου in 17β but also by the definite article with πνεῦμα.   Paul starts from the already developed concept πνεῦμα (which certainly does not represent a miraculous substance, see below, p. 74) and then goes on to explain that the κύριος *is* this πνεῦμα.   In other words, he takes over the popular view of the "spiritual body" of the ascended Redeemer, in order to express something which is right outside any material category.[2]

The decisive event thus has two moments: the raising up of Jesus, and the Parousia with the raising up of the faithful.   Consequently the Spirit is to be understood, as in the early Church, as a sign of that which is still to come. Now that the Resurrection of Jesus has come to pass, the Resurrection at the End of Time is no longer a vague hope; the reality of the Spirit's presence is a guarantee of the reality of what is to come.   Consequently Paul can describe the Spirit as the "first fruits", ἀπαρχή, of the still expected redemption of the Body (Rom. viii. 23), or as a "guarantee", ἀρραβών, for the new "house" which awaits us (II Cor. v. 5; i. 22.)[3].   Yet he is also able to adopt the view that the Spirit is the giver of extraordinary and miraculous feats.[4]

In I Thess. v. 19, for example, πνεῦμα, corresponding to προφητεῖαι, means a power which manifests itself in

[1] Cf. J. A. T. Robinson, *The Body*, 72.

[2] Scott, *op. cit.* 259–60, interprets thus: the κύριος (Christ) represents (i.e. means for the believer) the πνεῦμα.

[3] In all 3 cases, τοῦ πνεύματος is a Gen. of apposition (cf. Eph. i. 14), not a partitive genitive (Bl.-Debr. §167).

[4] The Gnostic would agree: but for him miracles are evidence for the new "spiritual" substance, while for the primitive Church, and especially for Paul, they are a foretaste of God's ultimate intervention.

exceptional ways.[1] The only question is whether the reference here is specifically to speaking with tongues; but II Thess. ii. 2 is certainly not to be understood in this way, since here the Spirit makes a particular statement. Eph. v. 18, it is true, probably refers to an ecstatic phenomenon, but v. 17 surely excludes speaking with tongues.[2] In I Cor. xiv. 37, as in xiv. 1 (cf. 12) πνευματικός is to be taken as a generic term, with προφήτης as one of its species. The same goes for I Thess. v. 19. Once (I Cor. xiv. 14–16) πνεῦμα occurs in antithesis to νοῦς as the miraculous power which bestows speaking with tongues; but then the emphasis lies only on the inadequacy of the νοῦς, and it may be that xiv. 15 is a way of expressing, not two alternatives, but (what was adequate for the congregation) the connection between πνεῦμα and νοῦς. In I Cor. ii. 4–5, ἀπόδειξις πνεύματος καὶ δυνάμεως is actually contrasted with σοφίας λόγοι and σοφία ἀνθρώπων, indeed in I Thess. i. 5 with λόγος altogether. In Rom. xv. 19 the δύναμις πνεύματος corresponds to δύναμις σημείων καὶ τεράτων.[3] In Gal. iii. 5 πνεῦμα corresponds to δυνάμεις.

In all this, the Spirit is consistently understood as something the possession of which can be demonstrated.[4] Thus Paul can count speaking with tongues among the activities of the Spirit just as much as gifts of healing or miraculous powers.[5] The formal similarity between these manifestations and the ecstatic phenomena of the heathen world is so far-reaching that Paul gives the Corinthians a criterion by which they can distinguish the activities of the Spirit of God from those which have a different source: the criterion is the confession of Jesus as Lord (I Cor. xii. 2–3).[6]

[1] Cf. J. Jeremias, Unknown Sayings of Jesus, E.T. 92.

[2] Dibelius, Gefangenschaftsbriefen³, ad loc.

[3] It is possible that by a chiastic construction λόγῳ should be understood here; but not in view of I Cor. ii. 4–5; iv. 20; I Thess. i. 5. (cf. II Cor. xii. 12).

[4] Gal. iii. 2; Dodd, Apostolic Preaching, 51–2.

[5] I Cor. xii. 9–10, 28–30; xiv. 18–26. Cf. Bultmann, T.N.T. I, 154–5.

[6] The same problem arises in the primitive church at large. I John iv. 2 makes the formula more precise. Matt. vii. 16; Didache xi. 7–12 find the criterion in the moral conduct of the prophet. Hermas, m. XI, 7–16, finds it besides in his positive attitude to the Church. Both these last

That Paul presupposes the existence of phenomena of this kind in Thessalonica just as much as in Galatia, in Rome (where he did not found the church) just as much as in Corinth, shows that this is something much more alive than a mere survival of a primitive attitude. Paul is more naïve than Luke; in the strictest sense he reckons all miraculous phenomena among the manifestations of the Spirit, not recognizing the late Jewish and Rabbinic limitation to the "Spirit of prophecy". Indeed the frequent role of the Spirit as a guarantee, ἀρραβών, of what is to come is much more prominent in Paul than in Luke.

When we were considering the "Hellenistic" concept of the spiritual body, with its emphasis on the here-and-now of the Spirit, we found that it had been significantly adapted so as to safeguard the not-yet. We find the same adaptation here, though the other way round. Not only does Paul, like Luke, hold fast to the belief that all the members of the Church are endowed with the Spirit[1] (Rom. viii. 9), but, unlike Luke, he attaches the greatest importance to a consequence he draws from this, namely that the manifestations of the Spirit need not necessarily have an extraordinary character. That is why, unlike the Corinthians, he includes among these manifestations "help", ἀντιλήμψεις and "administration", κυβερνήσεις,[2] and in other places "service", διακονία, and "acts of mercy", ἐλεεῖν, "contributions", μεταδιδόναι, and

---

passages at the same time allow for direct and startling appearances of the Spirit as a positive criterion. Ps.-Cor. (ed. Vetter, 1894) iii. ff. has recourse to the authority of the apostle. Ps.-Clem. *Hom.* ii. 6–11, mentions the occurrence of forecasts of the future as a proof of authenticity, cf. *Recog.* iv. 21.

[1] In certain passages πνευματικός seems to be restricted to a smaller group. Yet I Cor. xiv. 37 and Gal. vi. 1 should not be understood in this sense. I Cor. ii 13–iii. 3 calls πνευματικοί not a group of "ecstatics", but those who understand the gospel of the cross, so that all that is expressed in iii. 1–3 is that the believer may always be tempted to become an unbeliever (Scott, *op. cit.* 147–8). Nevertheless, the view that πνεῦμα is something exceptional is still so strong that οἱ πνευματικοί does not become a term for Church members like οἱ ἅγιοι, οἱ ἐν Χριστῷ.

[2] I Cor. xii. 28. Their absence from 29–30 shows that they were not among the gifts aspired to by the Corinthians.

"championing", προΐστασθαι (Rom. xii. 7–8). Still more significant is his notable depreciation of speaking with tongues,[1] which the Corinthians regarded as the most exceptional and indeed the highest of the gifts of the Spirit. This means that extraordinariness is felt to be basically irrelevant as a criterion; it would do just as well as a criterion for the religious experience of pagans (I Cor. xii. 2). The real criterion for measuring the value or lack of value of the gifts of the Spirit is the confession, Jesus is Lord, and at the same time the edification, οἰκοδομή, the expediency, συμφέρον, of the Church.[2] But this brings us to a completely new understanding of Spirit. (See below p. 80.)

2. Paul's personal interpretation

The argument has now taken a very individual turn. Paul had adopted the Hellenistic line of thought, which offered for the first time the simple and attractive possibility of interpreting spirit (πνεῦμα) quite simply as the new existence, and at the same time of seeing this in terms of union with the Redeemer. Yet he corrected any statements that savoured of natural religion, and by a line of thought which started from the Old Testament, he made it quite clear that salvation is not at man's disposal for him to possess. Yet even here Paul had to make qualifications. If the New Creation were already present, the Spirit could not be a mere sign for what was to come; it could not be something merely exceptional; it must be a feature of the new existence as such.

His new understanding of the Spirit allowed for both these points of view; but it was also moulded by another factor: the event which, for Paul, was the ultimate scandal, he could also understand as the ultimate saving event— that is, the cross.

---

[1] I Cor. xiv—though he esteems it for personal edification.
[2] I Cor. xiv. 3–5, 12, 26; xii. 7.

The argument in I Cor. ii. 6–16 starts from the premise that Paul has nothing to preach but Christ crucified (ii. 2). It is true that in the same passage Paul defines the Spirit as the miraculous power which transmits supernatural knowledge (σοφία ἐν μυστηρίῳ ἀποκεκρυμμένη, ii. 7, contrasted with ἀνθρωπίνη σοφία, ii. 13); yet he remains entirely true to that understanding of it for which the ground was prepared in a church influenced both by the Old Testament and by Hellenism. The miraculous power of the Spirit determines both the content and the form of the preaching, and is for that reason only perceptible to those who are "spiritual".[1] But what is the content of this "spiritual" teaching? Paul's reply is expressed in a way which is completely Gnostic: "the deep things of God", τὰ βάθη τοῦ θεοῦ (ii. 10); but its meaning is completely un-Gnostic: the saving work of God on the cross. Thus the content is "the gifts bestowed on us by God", τὰ ὑπὸ τοῦ θεοῦ χαρισθέντα ἡμῖν (ii. 12β); and the Wisdom of God (i. 24), which is revealed through the Spirit (ii. 7–10), is nothing other than Christ crucified (i. 23; ii. 2; confirmed in ii. 8)—which is "foolishness" (μωρία ii. 14) for the "unspiritual" (who are also those referred to in i. 23).[2] A Christian Gnostic could only have understood the cross as a tactical device for deceiving the demons and preventing them from obstructing the saving event of the Ascension.

This marks a decisive step forward. The cross is recognized as the crisis, now past, which separates the new creation from the old. Paul is a Hellenist in so far as he understands the Spirit as the power which releases men from "this age" (I Cor. ii. 6) and places them in the next. But at the same time he decisively redresses the balance: the union of the believer with the Lord is not given in a

---

[1] That ὅμοιον is only known to ὁμοίῳ can be paralleled in Empedocles fr. 109 (Diels⁷, I, 351, 20 ff.); Orph. Fr. 345 (Kern); Gnostics: Lietzmann, *Kor.*, *ad loc.*

[2] Kittel, art. *Gnosis*, E.T. 40. Cf. Thornton, *op. cit.* 108–9.

material mode of spirit, but in the knowledge, given only by the Spirit, of him who was crucified for us.[1]

It is now clear how Paul was able to take over the concept of the "spiritual body" of the Lord. All that is meant by "substance" is a way of conceiving the power which, for the Israelite, was the one reality; and all that the idea conveys is the insight that the believer's life depends entirely on his indissoluble union with the Lord, κύριος, in whom God's saving work has taken place for him. Entry into the "magnetic field" of the spirit-body then has no meaning in practice beyond the believer's self-abandonment into the "magnetic field" of the saving events, that is, of the Church which lives by the cross and resurrection. But at the same time there is no relaxation of the Old Testament attitude that the bearer of the Spirit is always completely dependent upon acts of God. His life does not depend upon this new substance, but upon the action of God on the cross. Thus it becomes possible to conceive of the Spirit as the basis of the believer's very existence, and no longer just as an extra miraculous power; yet at the same time it does not become a material possession of him whose nature it is to be saved, φύσει σωζόμενος. We can now understand how the extraordinariness of the manifestations can cease to be the decisive criterion. The supernatural quality of the knowledge does not depend on its being ecstatically received, or learnt, or on its being logically or illogically framed. The miracle is that a man can believe that, in Jesus Christ, God is on his side. The content of this supernatural knowledge is not some disclosure of the secrets of the heavenly places,[2] but is the love of God fulfilled in his action in the

[1] Dodd, *Apostolic Preaching*, 146–7, rightly stresses that a share in the Spirit is a share in Christ and not just in one of his gifts: though the passages he adduces for this (Rom. i. 4; II Cor. iii. 17) are capable of a purely natural interpretation.

[2] ἡμεῖς (I Cor. ii. 12) can only refer to all believers, as also in 10 (cf. Eph. iii. 18, where βάθος also occurs). βάθη τοῦ θεοῦ are picked up in 11 by τὰ τοῦ θεοῦ, and in 12 by τὰ . . . χαρισθέντα ἡμῖν (aorist!): therefore they must mean the already accomplished act of God's grace, and not something

6

cross, or else (a result of this) it is the fact that the believer is a son of God.[1]

So it is that πνεῦμα, Spirit, can be referred to outright as the Spirit of faith, πνεῦμα τῆς πίστεως (II Cor. iv. 13). Possessing the "earnest of the Spirit", ἀρραβὼν τοῦ πνεύματος, means "walking by faith", διὰ πίστεως περιπατεῖν (II Cor. v. 5, 7). In contrast to all secondary characteristics, it is the recognition and confession of Jesus as Lord which in I Corinthians xii. 3 is the gift most typical of the Spirit as such.

> The expression in Gal. iii. 14 (and v. 5?) which makes the reception of the Spirit depend upon faith (διὰ or ἐκ πίστεως)[2] appears to contradict this, but this is only superficial. The expression is used continually in opposition to "the works of the law", ἐξ ἔργων νόμου, and only means that it is not human merit which has earned the Spirit.[3] In Gal. v. 5 the content of what is received is the expectation of the ἔλπις δικαιοσύνης, that is, in fact, nothing other than faith understood in the light of the righteousness which has come to pass in Christ. This shows that the Spirit is not just an initial event.[4]

When the whole tradition is considered, it is understandable that Paul should see the operation of the Spirit more vividly in a continuous and externally guided "believing", πιστεύειν, than in the preliminary act of belief, πιστεῦσαι.[5] In a different way from Rom. viii. 16 Paul in Gal. iv. 6 can attribute to the Spirit not just

---

particular that lies in the future. λόγοις (13) can only be understood if the discussion in ii. 1–5 is still being carried on; and iii. 11, 18–23 shows that the argument has been continuous since i. 18. So iii. 1–3 (along with i. 7; iii. 16 *n.b.*) is to be understood as the paradox of the believer so often not living out what he believes (cf. viii. 7 with viii. 1; Rom. viii. 12–14 with viii. 9). In ii. 1 μυστήριον is probably the right reading, in which case it must be the same as in ii. 7.

[1] Rom. v. 5; viii. 16.

[2] In Gal. iii. 14: Lietzmann (*Gal. ad loc.*) renders: "the (fulfilment of the) promise, which is the πνεῦμα."

[3] In Gal. iii. 2, 5, the peculiar phrase ἀκοὴ πίστεως (not ἀκοῆς πίστις) may be used instead of πίστις simply because it is the work of the Spirit.

[4] Thus the first endowment of the Spirit has the aorist, its continued activity only the perfect (Thornton, *op. cit.* 82, on Rom. v. 5). Cf. ἐκ πίστεως εἰς πίστιν, Rom. i. 17.

[5] Hence there is no statement that the Spirit " gives " faith.

the recognition of sonship but concrete living as a Son of God; by which he simply affirms that the Spirit is not only a mysterious power which appears before faith and explains the birth of faith, but is also the power which continually reveals itself in faith.[1]

Incorporation into the Body of Christ, and the believer being made to drink of the Spirit (I Cor. xii. 13), is in the last analysis only what is expressed in I Cor. ii. 12 or Rom. viii. 16: it is the event which reveals and promises to a man the saving act of God in Christ Jesus, the event which makes him a Son of God and gives him life.[2] Since inclusion in the Body of Christ and inclusion in the saving events of the cross and resurrection (i.e. justification, δικαιωθῆναι) are ultimately the same thing, one can be ascribed to the Spirit just as much as the other (I Cor. vi. 11). The Name of the Lord justifies objectively, the Spirit subjectively. In the same way, being in the Spirit is synonymous with being in Christ. Both indicate the being of the believer. If he lives in contact with Christ's activity—who was crucified and resurrected for him—then he lives also in the sphere of the Spirit's activity, which reveals Christ to him and assures him of his salvation.[3] But since the Old Testament view made the believer dependent upon an always future act of God's grace, the gift of the Spirit appears now as a "waiting for the hope of righteousness" (Gal. v. 5), "walking in faith, not in sight" (II Cor. v. 7) a faith in the future resurrection (II Cor. iv. 13), a knowledge of the imminent redemption of the body (Rom. viii. 23), life everlasting (ζωὴ αἰώνιος Gal. vi. 8).

---

[1] That in Rom. i–v πίστις is predominant, and in vi–viii πνεῦμα, shows that, contrasted with the works of the Law, πίστις is the condition, and πνεῦμα the possibility, of the new existence.

[2] "Spirit-baptism" is therefore certainly not initiation into higher knowledge or equipment for special feats of strength (Flemington, *op. cit.* 56–7), but is subjection to God's saving act in Christ and so the foundation of all gifts of the Spirit (I Cor. xii. 4–11); hence it accompanies water-baptism. Cf. G. W. H. Lampe, *The Seal of the Spirit*, 56–7, 60.

[3] Rom. viii. 1, 9; cf. Bultmann, *T.N.T.* I, 334–6.

But if the Spirit is a divine power of which the main characteristic is not the extraordinariness of its activity, but the way in which it makes a man into a believer and governs his life as a believer, it can no longer be thought of as a power of magical operation, which a man is irresistably delivered over to.[1] It must be understood as the miraculous power of God which makes it possible for a man, who is separated from God, consciously and willingly to base his life on a power that is not his own.[2] But this indicates another line of development: although the two aspects cannot always be clearly distinguished, the Spirit is both the power which creates faith, and now also the norm of the life of faith. In so far as Paul wants to emphasize that the Spirit is entirely a gift of God, and not a potential of man himself, he conceives of it as power; but in so far as he wants to emphasize that it is the kind of power which summons to faith and not a substance which automatically makes a man divine, he conceives of the Spirit as the norm according to which the believer is called upon to live. This duality comes out most sharply in Gal. v. 25: "if we live by the Spirit, let us also walk by the Spirit". In the first clause it is established that the Spirit, as a superior power, determines a man's life; in the second clause the man is required consciously to recognize the fact and to allow his whole conduct to be governed by it.[3] Thus life in the Spirit has two sides. One, the negative side, is renouncing "the flesh", $\sigma\acute{\alpha}\rho\xi$; the other, the positive side, is laying oneself open to God and one's neighbour.

---

[1] In I Cor. xiv. 32 (cf. I Thess. v. 19) the believer is credited with control over the Spirit, in xiv. 1, 39 he is told to $\zeta\eta\lambda o\hat{\upsilon}\nu$ it, and warned not to $\kappa\omega\lambda\acute{\upsilon}\epsilon\iota\nu$ it; in Rom. xii. 6 the prophet is obliged to follow the faith proclaimed by the Apostle. The Spirit does not exclude rational deliberation (I Cor. vii. 40), the self (Rom. viii. 15–16) or the natural function of $\sigma\upsilon\nu\epsilon\acute{\iota}\delta\eta\sigma\iota\varsigma$ (Rom. ix. 1); and in I Cor. xiv. 14 the co-operation of $\nu o\hat{\upsilon}\varsigma$ is commended.

[2] In Pauline language, to renounce his $\kappa\alpha\acute{\upsilon}\chi\eta\mu\alpha$.

[3] Cf. the conjunction of ind. and imp. in Phil. iii. 16; Col. iii. 1, etc. Cf. Bultmann, $T.\mathcal{N}.T.$ I, 336–339.

(a) Renouncing the Flesh

The contrast between Spirit and "flesh" ($\sigma\acute{\alpha}\rho\xi$) originally, as in the Old Testament, means the opposition
between a force that is alien to man and man's own weak-
ness.[1] That is why God, or the Lord, $\kappa\acute{\upsilon}\rho\iota\sigma\varsigma$, his grace or
his pardon, appear in opposition to "flesh", and why in
Gal. iii. 2, 5 the Spirit is certainly understood mainly as
a miraculous power (see above p. 65). Now iii. 3 states
that the Galatians, having begun "in the Spirit" ($\pi\nu\epsilon\acute{\upsilon}\mu\alpha\tau\iota$)
were wanting to end "in the flesh" ($\sigma\alpha\rho\kappa\acute{\iota}$); this means,
in the first place, that they wanted to continue with their
own human strength. This is correct, but still inadequate;
for "flesh" corresponds to "works of the law", $\dot{\epsilon}\xi$ $\dot{\epsilon}\rho\gamma\omega\nu$
$\nu\acute{\omega}\mu\omega\upsilon$, Spirit to "hearing of the faith", $\dot{\epsilon}\xi$ $\dot{\alpha}\kappa\omega\hat{\eta}\varsigma$ $\pi\acute{\iota}\sigma\tau\epsilon\omega\varsigma$,
iii. 2, 5. If this antithesis is taken in its broad sense, and
not limited to moments of ecstasy and the supernatural,
the "Spirit" must at least be the power which determines the being of the believer as one whose life depends
on the fact of salvation. The meaning of "beginning in
the Spirit", $\pi\nu\epsilon\acute{\upsilon}\mu\alpha\tau\iota$ $\dot{\epsilon}\nu\acute{\alpha}\rho\chi\epsilon\sigma\theta\alpha\iota$, is then as follows. In the
indicative it expresses the certainty that a man's life
depends not on his own but on an alien strength. But
in the imperative it expresses a demand that he should
live his life relying upon that alien strength and not his
own, in other words that he should let the strength which
does in fact mould his life also be the standard at which
he aims. This comes out clearly in Phil. iii. 3. "Serving
the Spirit of God" ($\pi\nu\epsilon\acute{\upsilon}\mu\alpha\tau\iota$ $\theta\epsilon\omicron\hat{\upsilon}$ $\lambda\alpha\tau\rho\epsilon\acute{\upsilon}\epsilon\iota\nu$) means "not
trusting in the flesh" ($\omicron\dot{\upsilon}\kappa$ $\dot{\epsilon}\nu$ $\sigma\alpha\rho\kappa\grave{\iota}$ $\pi\epsilon\pi\omicron\iota\theta\acute{\epsilon}\nu\alpha\iota$) and 4–6 go
on to define "flesh" as the totality of characteristics and
deeds which a man could boast of as his own, that is, "his
own righteousness from the law" (iii. 9). "Spirit", by
contrast, is God's power, and therefore Christ's power.
Living under this power means also living up to this
standard and so "boasting in Jesus Christ" (iii. 3)—

[1] Hence the opposite to $\pi\nu\epsilon\hat{\upsilon}\mu\alpha$ can also be $\check{\alpha}\nu\theta\rho\omega\pi\omicron\varsigma$: I Cor. iii. 1–4;
Ign. *Eph.* v. 1 (Bultmann *T.N.T.* I, 153–54).

that paradoxical boasting of oneself which, when there is faith in Christ, leans only upon the "righteousness of God" given by Christ, and therefore esteems all personal advantages as refuse (iii. 8–9). In just the same way, we saw in I Cor. ii. 6–16 (see above) that the Spirit, when it is the miraculous power which gives to a man the knowledge of what God has done for his salvation, also demands from him renunciation of his own wisdom (ii. 1–5), indeed of all attention to human standards (14–15). Similarly, the Spirit in II Cor. iii. 6 appears mainly as the miraculous power which (in the future in I Cor. xv. 45 and so now in the present[1]) is credited with "making alive", $ζωοποιεῖν$. But iii. 9 shows that it is also the power which reveals to man what God has done for his salvation, enables him to live by it, and so gives him the possibility of not worrying about his own justification (see below pp. 91–2). Again, the phrase (Rom. ii. 29) "Circumcision of the heart in the Spirit and not in the letter" ($περιτομὴ καρδίας ἐν πνεύματι, οὐ γράμματι$) includes giving up all subservience to human criteria. Again, in Rom. vii. 5–6, "law" not only reveals or condemns sin, but actually provokes it, while the Spirit bestows the new "slavery" ($δουλεύειν$). The only difference (as comes out still more clearly in Rom. viii. 13) is that here that side of faith is emphasized which finds expression in concrete deeds (see below p. 77).

In Gal. iv. 23, 29 "he that is born of the Spirit" and "of the flesh" are opposed to each other. But in the second instance the word $γεννηθείς$ is lacking, and in iv. 23 $κατὰ πνεῦμα$ is replaced by $δι(ὰ τῆς) ἐπαγγελίας$; therefore there can be no thought of $πνεῦμα$ as a seed-like material of generation, still less of a feminine spirit which bears children like a mother-goddess. $δι(ὰ τῆς) ἐπαγγελίας$ is surely to be taken instrumentally. In iii. 18 $ἐπαγγελία$ is explicitly contrasted with $νόμος$[2] and in iv. 29

---

[1] I.e. "proleptic", not "realized" eschatology (H. V. Martin, *Proleptic Eschatology*, Exp. T. 51 (1939–40), 88–90).

[2] Cf. Rom. ix. 8 where $ἐπαγγελία$, instead of the usual $πνεῦμα$, is the opposite of $σάρξ$.

ὁ κατὰ σάρκα γεννηθείς is one who stands under the νόμος; it follows that the point of this passage is not to describe a miraculous birth, but to establish the fact that one son's life depends on human potentialities, the other's on the gift of God's grace. Once again, in this usage, cause and standard are intertwined. πνεῦμα means the gift of God's grace proceeding from Jesus Christ which sets in motion a new existence; and at the same time, that which is the standard according to which man lives out this existence. Whereas πνεῦμα had been principally the miraculous power which reveals God's saving work and so lays the foundation for a new life, so here its equivalence to ἐπαγγελία shows it in a still clearer light as the objective power, given by the grace of God, which creates this life (cf. John's view, below, pp. 91–2).[1]

In Gal. v. 17, man is apparently regarded as the neutral battlefield between flesh and Spirit. But v. 16, 18, show that even here there is no question of irresistible pressure. It is especially important to give due weight to ἵνα in 17; the intention of both must come into account. This means that even when a man is a believer he stands under the threat of apostasy just as much as under the promise of the Spirit. But it does not follow that both must work in him at once, or that he is delivered up to both without choice or freewill. What he is given is precisely the possibility of "walking in the Spirit", πνεύματι στοιχεῖν, with his flesh crucified (v. 24–5, see below, pp. 77–8). At the same time flesh is not actually a power external to man, but is his own will. No more is said here than that the flesh *can* become dominant and threaten him.

The Spirit in the sense of standard of life comes out clearly in Gal. vi. 8. Here, what determines a man's life is whether he "sows to the Spirit" or "sows to his own flesh". Similarly, in Rom. viii. 4–5 the formula "walking by the flesh" or "by the Spirit" is picked up by "setting one's mind on things of the flesh" or "of the Spirit", τὰ τῆς σαρκός, τὰ τοῦ πνεύματος φρονεῖν. This certainly

---

[1] Cf. ζωοποιεῖ, II Cor. iii. 6. Nevertheless, Paul's thought is expressed far more trenchantly in legal categories (πνεῦμα = ἀρραβών, ἀπαρχή, its activity = μαρτυρεῖν, δικαιοῦν) than in biological ones. So too the πνεῦμα υἱοθεσίας of Rom. viii. 15 is defined as that which proves (not begets) sonship.

brings out the paradox once again: the liberating "standard" of the Spirit is nothing else but the fact that God has acted and has achieved what the law was incapable of. So, in Gal. vi. 8, the word "own", ἑαυτοῦ, which stands with "flesh", is characteristically omitted with "spirit". This is only another way of saying that the standard of the Spirit, according to which a man directs his life, is not a potentiality of his own, but is given to him from outside himself.[1]

These two aspects are not altogether on the same plane. "Walking in the Spirit" is man's "yes" to the power of God which he cannot control and which, instead of his own power, must now determine his life. Therefore it is no accident that in Rom. viii. 13 "by the Spirit", πνεύματι, which indicates the motive power of this new life, is contrasted with "according to the flesh", κατὰ σάρκα, which expresses the standard. Still more clearly, Phil. iii. 3 speaks of "serving the Spirit *of God*", πνεύματι θεοῦ λατρεύειν, in distinction to "trusting in the flesh", πεποιθέναι ἐν σαρκί. Living "according to the Spirit", and being released from the flesh, means therefore just this: living in God's saving "sphere of action"—except that here the emphasis is more on the decision of the believer than on what happens to him. Yet even this decision of faith is understood as a gift of God, not as a man's own accomplishment; it is the standard by which he decides, and in fact also the power of his decision. Hence the notable pronouncement in Rom. viii. 4 that in consequence of the saving event the requirement of the law is fulfilled *in* (not by) those who walk after the Spirit and not after the flesh.[2] Still clearer is II Cor. i. 12, where the Grace of God (χάρις θεοῦ) is the opposite of fleshly activity. (Cf. Rom. v. 2.)

Thus we find ourselves in a world quite different from

[1] Cf. C. H. Dodd, *Romans*, 136–7, on Rom. viii. 28 ff.

[2] It is clearly the believer's concrete actions which matter here, but equally clearly these are based on *God's* power. In what follows, "abiding" is interpreted by strong active verbs.

that of the Gnostic. The Gnostic is certainly aware of the
same antithesis, but regards it as a datum of the universe;
whereas in Paul it is something created by the act of God in
Christ, in response to which man has to answer yes or no[1].

(b) Spirit as laying oneself open to God and one's neighbour

According to Rom. viii. 15, 26–7 and Gal. iv. 6, the
characteristic activity of the Spirit is Prayer.[2] This
connection is particularly underlined in Rom. viii. 27,
where the Spirit appears before God on behalf of man,
who left to his own does not even know what to pray for.[3]
The Spirit is therefore the same in its "ethical" function
as in its "soteriological": it proves to man his Sonship
(which is assured through God's saving act in Christ) and
enables him to live in it. Freedom from the old written
code, παλαιότης γράμματος, nevertheless means serving
the new code of the Spirit, δουλεύειν ἐν καινότητι πνεύματος.
The sinful passions which were aroused by the law must
be indulged no more (Rom. vii. 5–6). The requirement
of the law is fulfilled in those who now live according to
the Spirit instead of according to the flesh (Rom. viii. 4).
Setting the mind on the flesh (φρόνημα τῆς σαρκός) could
not be made to serve God's law (Rom. viii. 7); but
thanks to the Spirit, those who believe put to death the
deeds of the body (σῶμα, Rom. viii. 13). Living as a Son
of God can be summed up as faith made concrete.

The best example of this is in Gal. v. 13–15, where 13
and 16 make it clear that walking in the Spirit (πνεύματι
περιπατεῖν = ἐπιθυμίαν σαρκὸς μὴ τελέσαι) means being
servants of one another through love, διὰ τῆς ἀγαπῆς

---

[1] W. L. Knox, St. Paul and the Church of the Gentiles, 99, 109, 127, takes this
differently; but his view that πνεῦμα strengthens νοῦς (ib. 99) does not
allow for I Cor. xiv. 14.

[2] Never in the Rabbis (Str.-B. III, 243).

[3] This is not the Gnostic πνεῦμα which groans in its material prison
(cf. above, p. 21, n. 3), i.e. the innermost self of the "spiritual" man.
Similarly, Phil. i. 19 is to be translated "support through the Spirit"
(Dibelius, Phil. ad loc.). In this context it should be mentioned that in
Rom. xiv. 17, χαρά is a gift of the πνεῦμα.

δουλεύειν ἀλλήλοις, and so at the same time fulfilling the whole law (v. 14).[1] Love, so long as it is outward-looking, is nothing other than life in the Spirit, which has shaken itself free from trusting in the flesh. It is "active faith" (Gal. v. 6). The concrete result of it is the ful-filling of the law, precisely because man is relieved of straining after his own righteousness (v. 14–18).[2]

In other words, living in the power of the Spirit, and by the standard of the Spirit, means living in freedom from the law, living altogether "by Christ", "by grace", "by the cross", and at the same time being open to love (ἀγάπη). This comes out with particular force in Gal. v. 19–23. Whereas the evidence for the activity of the flesh is works (ἔργα), for the Spirit it is only possible to speak of "the fruits" (καρπός).[3] Not that "fruits" are only interior, invisible; it is clear from v. 25–vi. 10 (and indeed from v. 21β) that Paul is thinking entirely of concrete actions. Nevertheless they are all actions which cannot be *demonstrated* as being the activities of the Spirit.[4] Again, in I Cor. xiii. 1–3, it is neither the mira-culous nature of the deed nor the superhuman degree of sacrifice which is an unambiguous mark of love and of the Spirit which is expressed in it; yet it remains a fixed pre-mise that the Spirit, for example in worship (I Cor. xii–xiv), expresses itself in concrete loving activity. In Gal. v. 22, love, ἀγάπη makes its appearance as the first of the gifts of the Spirit,[5] and it is clear from Rom. xv. 30[6] and

---

[1] The opposite of σάρξ, instead of πνεῦμα, is here ἀγάπη.

[2] The contrast is between σάρξ (13, 16), νόμος (2–4, 18), περιτομή (6, 11), δουλεία (1) and πνεῦμα (5, 16–18), Χριστός (2–4), χάρις (4), σταυρός (11), ἀγάπη (6, 13) ἐλευθερία (1, 13). Hence νόμος appears again in antithesis to πνεῦμα (18); and contrariwise the activity of σάρξ is shown in the oppression and destruction of others (15).

[3] In Rom. vi. 21 καρπός is used *in malam partem*. It means a fortuitous instead of a procured result.

[4] That is why the plural φανερά is not used! φανέρωσις τοῦ πνεύματος I Cor. xii. 7 is its activity in the Church, but that cannot be calculated objectively—at any rate not by its exceptional character.

[5] Kittel, art. *Love*, E.T. 57.

[6] If indeed the parallel phrase in Philem. 9 is to be interpreted with Gal. v. 22 and not Rom. v. 5.

Col. i. 8, and especially from I Cor. xiii, that love
embraces all the others. But at this point it must be
reiterated that love can only be understood as faith when
it is directed towards others. In the same way, when the
Spirit appears as the power of sanctification (Rom. xv. 16;
I Cor. vi. 11, cf. II Thess. ii. 13) it is impossible to say
whether Paul wishes to emphasize the Spirit as involving
a man in God's saving activity and justifying him, or as
enabling him to base his life on it in concrete obedience.[1]
The two come to the same thing.[2]

At this point the difference in the Gnostic interpretation
becomes particularly apparent. When the Gnostic, in
ecstasy, possesses the Spirit, it destroys his individuality;
all that matters is the divine substance within him. It
also separates him from other men, who, if they are "unspiritual", are completely strange to him, and if they are
"spiritual", only serve to lead him to the point where he
finds himself (i.e. the same spiritual substance) in them.[3]
For him, the highest ideal is *Gnosis*, that is to say, the
apprehension of the divine substance within himself. And
it is precisely this which cuts a man off from others (cf. I
Cor. viii. 1–3). In Paul, on the other hand, knowledge
($\gamma\nu\tilde{\omega}\sigma\iota\varsigma$) is subordinate to love ($\dot{\alpha}\gamma\dot{\alpha}\pi\eta$).[4] In other words,
if the knowledge which is given by the Spirit is
knowledge of the saving act of God, then it frees man from
himself and in so doing lays him open to others. At the
same time it restores to him anew his individuality, not in
such a way that he can contemplate it and take his stand
upon it before God and man, but as a means of existing
for others.

Thus it is the concept of the Church which really

---

[1] The first is stressed in I Cor. vi. 11, the second in I Cor. vi. 19; II Cor.
vi. 6; I Thess. iv. 7–8 (cf. Rom. xiv. 17).
[2] C. T. Craig, *Paradox of Holiness*, Interpretation, 8 (1952), 147–61.
There is no neutral zone between flesh and spirit; therefore freedom from
sin is necessarily obedience.
[3] Hence the "spiritual" Gnostic founds, at most, $\theta\dot{\iota}\alpha\sigma\sigma\iota$, not permanent
$\dot{\epsilon}\kappa\kappa\lambda\eta\sigma\dot{\iota}\alpha\iota$.
[4] Kittel, art. *Gnosis*, E.T. 43.

decides the matter. When Paul speaks of being received into the "Body of Christ" (probably adopting a Hellenistic expression) this serves to underline the unity of the Body, which binds the various members together.[1] The value of spiritual gifts is not to be found in the fact that they mark out their bearers as "spiritual people", but that they build up the Church (I Cor. xiv). It is true that the building-up happens through the "spiritual", but then *everyone* is "spiritual", everyone has his χάρισμα. If individuals break away, they thereby show themselves to be "unspiritual", σαρκικοί.[2]

It is true, then, that the Spirit is still the miraculous power which proceeds entirely from God and breaks in upon man's affairs in a way quite out of his control. But Paul has carried this to its logical conclusion. Precisely because it is the power of God, it cannot be exhibited in a series of exceptional events. If it could, man would be able to appeal to his own religious and miraculous powers. Basically, it is the power which involves him in the saving act of God through Christ, takes away his independence, makes impossible for him all confidence in his own "flesh" (σάρξ) and lays him open to a life of love (ἀγάπη). All that Paul has done is to carry to their logical conclusion the synoptics' interpretations of the cross: sin-offering for many (Mark, xiv. 24, see above p. 68); call to repentance, shattering all false religious security (Mark xii. 1–12, see above p. 73); event which makes possible the discipleship of service (διακονία, Mark x. 45, see above p. 77).

This is different from the way in which Acts sees it; certainly not because Paul introduces ethical categories; nor yet because in Acts it is the outward history of the Church, in Paul the inner life of the individual, which is

[1] Rom. xii. 4–5; I Cor. xii. 13–27; x. 17; Gal. iii. 28. Being involved in God's saving act means death to everything of which a man can boast and which can separate him from others.

[2] I Cor. iii. 3–4. Hence the Church is not subject to individual πνευματικοί, but can pass judgment on them.

controlled by God; nor again because in Acts the possession of the Spirit can be ascertained while in Paul it is a part of faith; nor yet because the dynamic conception of the Spirit in Acts is in contrast with Paul's "being in Christ". At most these are superficial differences, underlying which we can see a deeper difference: the Spirit is the power of God which enables men to believe in the Cross and Resurrection of Jesus. This means that, when its other-ness needs to be emphasized, it can have the dynamic appearance of an extraordinary and miraculous power; but it can also be at the root of a permanent life in Christ. It can control both the outward fortune of the Church and the inner life of the individual; it can be visible or invisible, momentary or permanent. But in all this it is no longer merely an additional phenomenon, as in Acts; it is the power which determines the new life of faith as such.

3. *The Spirit and Christ*

In Rom. viii. 1–11, "the Spirit of God in you", πνεῦμα θεοῦ ἐν ὑμῖν (9), alternates with "Christ in you", Χριστὸς ἐν ὑμῖν (10), and "you . . . in spirit", ὑμεῖς ἐν πνεύματι (9), with "those who are in Christ" τοῖς ἐν Χριστῷ (1), without any apparent difference in meaning.[1] From the Hellenistic standpoint this can be explained as a matter of terminology; the ascended Christ has the substance of Spirit (cf. above p. 57); consequently, abiding in Christ here and now is equivalent to abiding in the Spirit, and in the same way Christ's abiding in us is equivalent to the Spirit's abiding in us. It can be objected to this that "in the Spirit" (ἐν πνεύματι)[2] often occurs in an instrumental sense; but this objection collapses as soon as it is realized that the concept of the substantial sphere which the believer enters is only Paul's formal way of

[1] Further parallels in W. D. Davies, *Paul and Rabbinic Judaism*, 178.
[2] Rom. xv. 13; I Thess. i. 5. Alternation between ἐν . . . and the dative: I Cor. xii. 3/xiv. 2 (cf. Eph. i. 13/iv. 30; v. 18). Dative for local ἐν: Gal. iii. 3; v. 5, 16, 25.

grasping the concept of power. However, it follows
that this approach can only explain why this particular
terminology is chosen. It cannot explain the reality
behind it. In its context, "walking by the Spirit"
(περιπατεῖν κατὰ πνεῦμα) or "having the mind of the
Spirit" (φρονεῖν τὰ τοῦ πνεύματος) is referred back to
"being in the Spirit" (εἶναι κατὰ πνεῦμα, 4–5, or ἐν
πνεύματι, 9) and this in turn is referred to "the dwelling"
of the Spirit "in you" (9).[1] This makes it clear yet
again (cf. above p. 69) that Paul is trying to define
the conception of the "sphere" in which the believer
lives in terms of what it means to him, that is, as a
power into whose range we have come, and which
determines our thinking (φρονεῖν), our walking (περιπατεῖν)
and our obedience to the law of God (ὑποτάσσεσθαι τῷ
νόμῳ τοῦ θεοῦ).

This power is not something nameless and unknown.
It is identical with the ascended Lord—so long as one does
not think of the ascended Lord in himself, but only in his
dealings with the Church.[2] Paul is hardly touched by the
metaphysical question how God, Christ and the Spirit
are related to each other. For this reason at least it is a
mistake to see the root meaning of the word for Paul as
"the third person of the Trinity". The Spirit often makes
a completely impersonal appearance (I Cor. xii. 13;
I Thess. v. 19); it can alternate with Wisdom or Power
(I Cor. ii. 4–5, 13). The Spirit which is given to man can
be referred to as "his spirit" or as the "spirit of sonship".
The Spirit "teaches", "thinks", etc., but it shares this
property with other words like "wisdom" or "flesh".
The question of how far the Spirit is personal may be a

---

[1] From the O.T. point of view, this view is more surprising than the
other, which is at least grounded on the concept of the Spirit "clothing" a
man (L. Köhler).

[2] Paul is not the first to make this distinction (C. A. A. Scott, *Christianity
according to St. Paul*, 141–5. In Acts the Spirit is not only τοῦτο (ii. 33)
in distinction from the Pauline and Johannine (John xiv. 26) ἐκεῖνος, but
πνεῦμα and κύριος alternate (see above, p. 39 top).

false one,[1] for the simple reason that the word "personal" does not exist in either Greek or Hebrew. Paul shares with Judaism (see above p. 11) and with the early Christian Church (see above p. 36) the conception of the Spirit as the gift and power of the Last Age. His concern is not to replace the concept of "power" by the concept of "person", but to show that this power is not an obscure "something" but is the way and manner in which the Lord of the Church is present. For that reason the Spirit can be placed on a level with the Lord, or subordinated to him, quite indifferently (II Cor. iii. 17–18, see above p. 60).[2] For that reason also, Paul can occasionally use God, Lord and Spirit interchangeably, simply because their encounter with the believer always takes one and the same form.[3] The clearest instance of this is I Cor. xii. 4–6, not only because all three concepts there correspond to each other, but also because the Spirit, as it is manifested in the life of the Church, is defined precisely as the "manifestation of the Spirit", φανέρωσις τοῦ πνεύματος (7), and is distinguished from the source of this activity.

A question remains about II Cor. xiii. 13. Is κοινωνία τοῦ ἁγίου πνεύματος a subjective or objective genitive? Similar passages in I Cor. i. 9, Phil. iii. 10 suggest that it is objective, but the arguments for this interpretation are by no means convincing.[4] The nearest parallel in Phil. ii. 1 is certainly not to be understood as fellowship with the Holy Spirit of God; for κυρίου and θεοῦ are certainly subjective genitives. It is then open to question, whether the meaning is not completely parallel: "the κοινωνία given by the Spirit". But this still does not help us to decide whether it is brotherly fellowship

---

[1] Cf. C. Welch, *The Holy Spirit and the Trinity*, Theology Today, 8 (1951–2) 33.

[2] Similarly it can be almost synonymous with θεός (I Cor. iii. 16; cf. xiv. 25; II Cor. vi. 16) and yet be contrasted with θεός (I Cor. ii. 10; Rom. viii. 26–7).

[3] E. Lewis, *The Biblical Doctrine of the Holy Spirit*, Interpretation, 7 (1953), 281–98 shows that both in O.T. and N.T. the Spirit is often replaced by God, Lord, etc., without any difference of meaning.

[4] Cf. J. E. L. Oulton, *Holy Spirit and Holy Communion*, 62–4; G. J. Jourdan, *KOINΩNIA in I Cor. x. 16*, J. B. L. 67 (1948), 116–18.

one with another which is in question, or fellowship with the Spirit. This last corresponds better with χάρις and ἀγάπη and would give κοινωνία the strongly active sense of the gift by the Spirit of a share in itself, in which case the first meaning would be included. In other words, it comes to the same thing if one explains the expression as an objective genitive. However, it is better to interpret κοινωνία τοῦ ἁγίου πνεύματος as a subjective genitive, so long as the complexity of the notion is grasped; for in fact the objective reality of this fellowship characterizes it just as strongly as the subjective power which bestows it.[1]

All these concepts occur again in Rom. v. 1–5, Gal. iv. 4–6, this time not in exact parallel, but all close together. These passages show that God's work in the Son or in the Spirit must always be understood as really the work of God himself, but that the question, how God, Lord and Spirit are related to each other, is not yet felt to be a question at all.

4. *The Human Spirit*

What Paul says about this is by no means consistent or even original. The Holy Spirit of God affects the whole man, and cannot be given a psychological explanation; a fact which enables Paul to take over popular conceptions without embarrassment. The thesis that Paul knows nothing of a human spirit cannot be sustained. Along with "body" and "flesh", "spirit" appears to be simply a general word for the functions of the human soul (I Cor. vii. 34; II Cor. vii. 1; Col. ii. 5?): thus it can be used as equivalent to "soul" (ψυχή, Phil. i. 27, see below p. 100) or, like "flesh" (σάρξ), can describe the whole man; the only difference being that in this case the soul is emphasized more than the body (II Cor. ii. 13; vii. 5; cf. vii. 13; I Cor. xvi. 18, always with personal pronouns). In closing greetings (Gal. vi. 18; Phil. iv.23; Philem. 25)

---

[1] Jourdan, *op. cit.* 119, 123–4. Cf. L. S. Thornton, *The Common Life in the Body of Christ*, 74–5.

"your spirit" means exactly the same as "you" (I Thess. v. 28). In the same way, in I Cor. ii. 11 "spirit" can stand for human consciousness and be distinguished from the Spirit of God which exactly corresponds to it; although in this case it is precisely the correspondence which determines the use of the words. So, too, in the famous passage I Thess. v. 23, spirit, along with soul and body, is to be taken as a component part of man, on the lines of popular psychology.[1]

Paul, therefore, has no scruples about taking over "spirit" as a psychological term from current Jewish usage. Yet even so he still regards it as being the spirit which is God's gift and so ultimately alien to man. He does not need to stress this point, and is capable of ignoring it altogether, but sometimes it comes out quite clearly. In I Cor. xiv. 14 the spirit which is given to a "spiritual" person—which is clearly distinguished from his mind ($\nu o \hat{v} s$)—can still be referred to as "his" spirit. In Rom. i. 9, too, the "Spirit" is the Spirit of God which is made available to the apostle personally.[2]

> I Cor. v. 3-5 is not altogether clear. The spirit of the sinner, which must be saved, is certainly the "I" which is given him by God, and so a part of the Spirit of God; although it represents also the totality of the new man, the believer.[3] But at the same time it is not a *character indelebilis*; for Paul allows for the possibility that it may be lost, that is, if the judgment on the $\sigma \acute{a} \rho \xi$ is not carried out (does this mean illness? or death? xi. 30 cf. Acts v. 1-11). It is the new "I" of a man which would be lost if he gave up altogether being a Christian. To avoid this last, horrible, ultimate possibility becoming actual,

[1] Above, p. 22-3. The greeting is very likely traditional, if not liturgical, and so tells us little about Paul's conception of man (Dibelius, *Thess.*[3], *ad loc.*). The combination may be fortuitous, as in Deut. vi. 5 (W. Robinson, q. by J. A. T. Robinson, *The Body*, 27, n. 2).

[2] Cf. Rom. xii. 11; in Rom. viii. 10-11 the divine origin of the Spirit is strongly emphasized.

[3] It is certainly not simply the human soul; for Paul is never concerned with the saving of a mere soul. It is the man himself in the existence Christ has given him, not in his natural powers and potentialities (cf. iii. 15, $a \mathring{v} \tau \acute{o} s$).

the purifying judgment on the σάρξ must take place.[1]   In which case the apostle's own spirit, both here and in Colossians ii. 5, must also be understood as the gift of the Spirit of God imparted to him, which guarantees his authority and reaches out even beyond his bodily presence.

It is significant that this spirit, which abides in a man, is not suggested as being in any way more than something that is both attached to him and related to God.   Moreover, it never means the soul completed by God's Spirit. It is true that Paul unthinkingly uses spirit almost in the sense of soul; but this is only common Judaic usage which he naturally cannot avoid using himself.[2]   Paul never says that the soul finds its completion in spirit.   Where he does actually mention the idea of an "organ" which receives the Spirit of God, he also calls it "spirit" and expressly describes it as something not belonging to man but given to him by God (Rom. viii. 15–16; I Cor. ii. 11).[3]   When Paul is being consciously precise, he contrasts, like the Gnostics, this individual, transcendent, essentially divine spirit with both soul and body.[4]   A positive advantage of this is that "spirit" is sharply distinguished from the human "mind" (νοῦς, I Cor. xiv. 14); and the negative side of it comes out in Paul's avoidance of the word "spirit" when he wants to describe the profoundest "I" of pre-Christian man.[5]

At first sight this state of affairs is bewildering, but it becomes clear when it is realized that Paul's thought proceeds entirely from the *activity* of the Spirit of God, and that he regards the whole existence of the believer as

[1] The σάρξ which is destroyed is not Sin (F. Grosheide, *I Cor.* 123, *ad loc.*). Cf. I Pet. iv. 1, 6, 17, and below, p. 102 (iv).

[2] The human spirit is never thought of in the Stoic sense as an offshoot of God's Spirit, although Gen. ii. 7 might have suggested this.

[3] Cf. Odes of Solomon vi. 7.

[4] See below p. 87 ; N. H. Snaith, *The Distinctive Ideas of the O.T.* 184–6 ; F. C. Synge, *The Holy Spirit and the Sacraments*, Scottish J. of Th. 6 (1953), 68–69.   The dualism of immanence-transcendence is superseded by the πνεῦμα which comprises both.

[5] For which he uses ἐγώ or νοῦς (Rom. vii. 17–23).

determined by it. For Paul, the Spirit of God is no extraordinary magic power; it reveals to the believer the saving work of God in Christ, and enables him to give responsible and informed assent to it (see above p. 67 and especially p. 72). Consequently, the Spirit remains entirely God's, and is never merged in the Spirit which is given to the individual;[1] yet at the same time it can be the deepest "I" of the man whose life no longer proceeds from his own being , but from God's being on his behalf.

Appendix: πνευματικός

Paul's language becomes pointed when he contrasts the πνευματικοί with the ψυχικοί. In I Cor. ii. 13–15 πνευματικός means the man who in the power of God's Spirit acknowledges God's saving work (see above pp. 68–9), while the ψυχικός is blind to it.[2] This contrast is at its sharpest here, because Paul does not recognize any neutral existence. If you do not have the Spirit of God, you are controlled by the spirit of the world, πνεῦμα τοῦ κόσμου.[3] There is an equally pointed distinction in I Cor. xv. 44–46 between the σῶμα πνευματικόν and the σῶμα ψυχικόν (cf. above p. 62) which shows that even before Paul these terms had been coined and were current.[4] It follows from what has just been said that πνευματικά can be the content of the knowledge which is only given through the Spirit of God, that is, heavenly things inaccessible to the νοῦς, in other words the gospel of Christ (I Cor. ii. 13; ix. 11; Rom. xv. 27). In these two last passages, earthly things are subsequently mentioned as carnal (σαρκικά) though without any connotation of evil. They are simply what promotes the natural life but does not unite with God. Thus even ordinary foods and drinks are contrasted with the

---

[1] Rom. viii. 16, cf. Bultmann, *T.N.T.* I, 206–7.
[2] So Jude 19 (see below, pp. 102–3).
[3] A mythological expression, as in Eph. ii. 2. On iii. 1–3 and I Cor. xiv. 37, Gal. vi. 1, see above, p. 66, n. 1.
[4] Cf. above, pp. 22–23.

"spiritual" ones which come directly from God's world and bestow divine power (I Cor. x. 3). There is no idea here of the elements bearing the Spirit, as is shown by passages using similar language[1] and also by I Cor. x. 4β.[2] In I Cor. xiv. 1 πνευματικά means the totality of spiritual gifts.[3] In Rom. vii. 14, the law (νόμος) is referred to as πνευματικός; this is to make it clear that it is God's law, νόμος θεοῦ, and proceeds not from man's world, but from God's.[4]

D. JOHN

1. *The significance of eschatology*

While the saying handed down in John xxi. 22 still represents the conviction of Mark ix. 1; I Thess. iv. 17, that some people will live to see the Parousia, and while the scoffers are already beginning to scoff (II Peter iii. 4; I Clem. xxiii. 2–3; II Clem. xi) and their opponents are simply deferring the time of the Parousia (II Peter iii. 8–10; I Clem. xxiii. 4–5; Barn. xxi. 3),[5] John on the one hand is firmly convinced that the consummation is still to come,[6] but he also proclaims, more clearly even than Paul, the present actuality of the salvation which is one day to be consummated. So that the first difference from the synoptics and from Paul appears in the greater consistency with which the old concepts are subjected to revision.

[1] I Pet. ii. 5. Also Barn. xvi. 10 ("spiritual" temple contrasted with one made with hands, perishable, 7, 9); Did. x. 3 ("spiritual" food and drink contrasted with ordinary ones); Ign. *Eph.* v. 1 ("spiritual" relationship with the Bishop). Cf. C. F. D. Moule, *Sanctuary and Sacrifice in the Church of the N.T.*, J.T.S. N.S. 1 (1950), 34–5 (spiritual=repudiation of external ritual).

[2] The "Spiritual Rock" is unearthly, miraculous, proceeding from God's world.

[3] Also xii. 1. Cf. Rom. i. 11.

[4] Rom. vii. 22, 25. Similarly Eph. i. 3. On all this see also Selwyn, *I Peter*, 281–5.

[5] C. K. Barrett, *The Holy Spirit in the Fourth Gospel*, J.T.S. N.S. 1 (1950) 2–3; *idem*, *The Gospel according to St. John*, ad loc.

[6] vi. 27; xii. 25; xiv. 2–3; xvii. 24. xi. 24, though inadequate, is not contradicted. Cf. E. Schweizer, *The Reinterpretation of the Gospel by the Fourth Evangelist*, Interpretation, 8 (1954), 387–96. On the whole question cf. W. F. Howard, *Christianity according to St. John*, 106–128.

In John there is no conception of a sudden appearance of the Spirit or of the exceptional character of its manifestations, or indeed of ecstatic phenomena or miracles altogether.[1] Jesus, again, never appears as a man of the Spirit. His inspired discourse and his miracles are never ascribed to the Spirit.[2] The way trodden by Luke is not adequate for John. He abandons completely the concept of inspiration, since it only serves to express a basic separation between God and Jesus which must ever be overcome by a third entity, namely the Spirit. But if the Christ-event is really to be understood as the turn of the era, then it is all-important that it is the Father himself, and not just a gift of the Father's, which is encountered in Christ. It follows naturally that the stories of his conception by the Spirit, and of his endowment with the Spirit at baptism, are left out.

> The first one is corrected straight away in i. 13;[3] though the verse shows that for John conception by the Spirit does exist, not for the Son, but for believers. The descent of the Spirit on Jesus in i. 33 is mentioned only as a proof, not as a cause, of Jesus' Sonship.

2. *Spirit as opposed to "flesh": a sphere*

Other differences from Paul are not fundamental but arise from the fact that John's thought is cast less in the categories of Rabbinic than of a heterodox Judaism. To the latter belongs the pre-Pauline usage (cf. above p. 57) by which "spirit" and "flesh" distinguish the divine from the earthly sphere (iii. 6; vi. 63). While iii. 6 speaks of "being born of the Spirit", iii. 3 and i. 13 speak of being

---

[1] Pentecost happens without tongues of fire or rushing winds, xx. 22–3 (Barrett, J.T.S. 1950, 3–4). And in xvi. 13 there is no trace of the old view that the main gift of the prophetic πνεῦμα is foresight (Barrett, *St. John*, *ad loc.*).

[2] E.g. vii. 28, 37; xii. 44; v. 8; vi. 11; ix. 6–7; xi. 43. Again, in xi. 33; xiii. 21, it is not the spasm of a "spiritual" man which is described; πνεῦμα is purely psychological=ἑαυτόν (xi. 33, cf. Barrett, J.T.S. 1950, 3). In xix. 30 it means the physical life-force.

[3] Howard, *op. cit.* 66–8.

born "from above" or "from God". The opposite of
"being of God" (εἶναι ἐκ τοῦ θεοῦ) is being "of below"
(ἐκ τῶν κάτω), "of the devil", "of the world",[1] just as the
opposite of "born of the Spirit" is "born of the flesh"
(iii. 6). In other words "Spirit", "above", "God" seem
to correspond to "flesh", "below", "devil", "world".

iv. 24 states the equation: God is Spirit.[2] In this
sentence John proclaims that the eschatological hour, in
which "above" and "below", spirit and flesh, God and
the world, meet together—that this hour, however much
its consummation is still pending, has already struck.[3]
Greek and Gnostic thought envisaged an ultimate union
between the divine substance and the originally similar
substance buried in mankind. John proclaims the exact
opposite, namely that it is in the historical man Jesus of
Nazareth that God calls us to faith and comes to meet us.
Worshipping God in Spirit and in truth no longer means
worshipping in the consciousness of one's own "spiritual
substance", still less in one's own spirituality as opposed to
anything external; it means worshipping in the divine
and no longer in the worldly sphere, in reality and no
longer in the sphere of appearances. But this sphere is
only to be found where God himself enters the world, that
is, in him who is the true God, ὁ ἀληθινὸς θεός (I
John v. 20).[4] There were many objections to ritual worship;[5] and to put it in a neat formula, one could say that

[1] viii. 23, 42–7; xv. 19; xvii. 14, 16.

[2] Yet John avoids the expression νοῦς, and gives to the term πνεῦμα
a completely new meaning by opposing it absolutely to σάρξ. This
radical other-ness of God over against everything human is O.T., not
Greek, in feeling.

[3] Cf. Barrett, J.T.S. 1950, 6. *Idem, St. John, ad loc.* understands πνεῦμα
here as life-giving power of God, whereas ἀλήθεια stresses the connexion
with the historical Jesus. It would be more exact to define it as the power
which forges union with God's world (and is therefore life-giving).

[4] Cf. i. 9; vi. 32–35; x. 11; xv. 1; x. 30; xiv. 9–10. In fact, xiv. 26 (not
the D reading!) and xvi. 12–13 give us the key: the Spirit is the elucidation
of the Incarnation (O. Cullmann, *Early Christian Worship*, E.T. 72).

[5] I Kings viii. 27. Cf. Sen. *Epistulae*, xli. 1–2 (cf. lxvi. 12). "Do not
lift your hands to heaven . . . God is near you, with you, in you . . . a holy
spirit dwells in you."

John iv. 24 orientates true worship upon the flesh and blood of Jesus.[1] Spirit consequently does not mean the soul and the understanding of man, what is "nearest to God in man" something immaterial, "completely inward".[2] Like "truth," it means the reality of God. In form, it is Hellenistic and substantial; but in fact it is completely suffused by the knowledge that this reality is only to be found in Jesus. Seeing the truth means seeing in Jesus Him who is truly God (τὸν ἀληθινὸν θεόν viii. 32; xvii. 3). "In Spirit" (ἐν πνεύματι) therefore comes to the same as Paul's "in Christ". The sovereign act of God's revelation in Jesus has marked out the area in which true worship takes place. Consequently any cult which is not a gift resulting from this act of God—however "spiritual" it may be—is condemned as not taking place "in the Spirit".[3]

3. Spirit as opposed to "flesh": a life-giving power

As in John iv. 23–4, so also in iii. 3–5 "Spirit" appears as the divine world which is inaccessible to man so long as he does not live "in the Spirit", ἐν πνεύματι. But here this life is connected with "being born of the Spirit".[4]

The decisive question in John is this: how does one obtain *life, ζωή*? Paul too could ask this question and, like John, he could answer that only the "Spirit" πνεῦμα, is responsible for making alive, ζωοποιεῖν (John vi. 63;

[1] Hoskyns, *Fourth Gospel, ad loc.*

[2] Howard, *op. cit.* 61; G. H. C. McGregor, *John* (Moffatt N.T. Commentary), *ad loc.* On ἀλήθεια see Bultmann, *T.N.T.* II, 18–19.

[3] The opposition between the spirit of truth, knowledge, light, and error, malice, darkness has its roots in pre-Gnostic Judaism. See above, p. 15ff. and Test. Jud. xx. 1; *Damascus Document,* ii. 13 (ii. 10). πνεῦμα ἀληθείας ought not therefore to be taken in in the O.T. sense: "Spirit of faith" (cf. *contra* N. H. Snaith, *The Distinctive Ideas of the O.T.,* 181).

[4] The Spirit is begetter, not mother, i. 13; I John iii. 9. This corresponds to the Aristotelian proposition, that every nature begets its own substance (*M.M.* I, 10, 1187a, 31). It is not simply an extension of Rom. vi. 3–4; I Cor. xv. 45, or a transference of Ps. ii. 7 from Jesus to believers (cf. *contra* C. F. Burney, *Aramaic Origin of the Fourth Gospel,* 45; Howard, *op. cit.* 198). On the question of new birth, cf. Dibelius, *Past.*[3] on Tit. iii. 5; *idem, Jak.* on i. 18; C. H. Dodd, *Fourth Gospel,* 303–4.

II Cor. iii. 6). But Paul thinks in the Rabbinic category of justification, δικαιοσύνη,[1] and consequently defines life, ζωή, straight away in terms of "righteousness", δικαιοσύνη, as opposed to "judgment", κατάκρισις (see above, p. 71). For John, on the other hand, life, ζωή, consists in knowing, γινώσκειν, God (xvii. 3).[2] Therefore he does not follow Paul's line of thought all the way, for this would imply that the Spirit gives (a) life (because it communicates the knowledge of God's redeeming act on the cross, see above p. 69), and therefore (b) freedom from boasting (καύχημα) (see above, p. 73), and therefore (c) openness to one's neighbour (see above, pp. 77–81), in short (d) δικαιοσύνη in its largest sense. Consequently John can make far more direct use of the concept of the life-giving Spirit (which was originally conceived along quite different lines) without thereby saying anything fundamentally different from Paul. As in Paul, the originally substantial conception is completely superseded. The only difference from Paul is that union with the Redeemer itself entails the abolition of the separation between God and man,[3] and for this reason Spirit—more than in Paul—refers to God's world (as opposed to σάρξ) as the sphere from which man is controlled in his new existence. John therefore has less embarrassment than Paul in ascribing birth, γεννᾶν, to this world of God's. But this no longer means any change in the substance of the soul;[4] it now means the God-given knowledge that in Jesus God himself has come into the world; and this is made a reality by faith. iii. 3–5 is a statement of the theme that knowledge of this kind can only be a gift of God and in no way a possibility for man on his own: it is also a challenge to Nicodemus to stop worrying about

[1] Kittel, art. "Righteousness". E.T. 72–3.

[2] The noun γνῶσις does not occur at all, presumably in opposition to "Gnostic" usage. But the verb is frequent.

[3] Hence the Cross is not seen primarily as expiation, but as the consummation of the Incarnation, in which God's loving approach to the κόσμος is completed (cf. Dodd. op. cit. 441–2).

[4] A. L. Humphries, The Holy Spirit in Faith and Experience, 235–6.

what is possible *for him* but to lay himself right open to the gift of God—in other words, to believe.

In iii. 8 πνεῦμα means *wind*.[1] Nevertheless the wind, being intangible and uncontrollable, corresponds to the Spirit of God. But it is important to see that it is not the Spirit, but the bearer of the Spirit, who is described in this way. Special emphasis is now laid on the "strangeness" of him who is born of the Spirit. The believer, whose going and coming is unknown to the world,[2] is no longer accessible to human knowledge, and although faith will certainly express itself in acts of love (ἀγάπη), nevertheless "being born of the Spirit" does *not* mean moral renewal. It is something unobservable, whether in its activity or its appearance, whether in its suddenness, the spasm of repentance which precedes it, or the feeling of liberation. It is that happening which the world can now neither measure nor judge.

In vi. 63 (cf. xv. 3) πνεῦμα, in contrast to σάρξ which profiteth nothing, is credited with a γεννᾶν which proceeds from the words spoken by Jesus as the Son of Man. It follows from vi. 51–8 that σάρξ here can only mean the flesh of the Incarnate One which becomes most scandalously visible in the Eucharist in its saving necessity for men. Nothing is said of the identity of Jesus' σάρξ with the Eucharistic elements. What is emphasized is only that in the Eucharist the individual must take concrete advantage of the sacrifice of Jesus as it is proclaimed in the saying over the Bread. For John, the one purpose of Baptism and Lord's Supper is to give evidence for the Incarnation.[3] The force of vi. 63 is then that this σάρξ is only profitable when the πνεῦμα gives the knowledge that it is precisely in this σάρξ that ζωή is to be found.[4] Following viii. 15, the explanation now runs

[1] Linguistically, from *πνεϝω. In LXX, cf. Jonas iv. 8; Jer. iv. 11. Another view: T. M. Donn, *The Voice of the Spirit* (John iii. 8), Exp. T. 66 (1954–5), 32.

[2] Cf. vii. 27–8; viii. 14; ix. 29; xv. 19.

[3] It is certainly true that for the believer this scandal is converted into grace and help (Barrett, *St. John, ad loc.*).

[4] Cf. *contra* McGregor, *op. cit.* 161–2, who sees material communion in 51γ–58, spiritual communion in 63. Dodd, *Fourth Gospel*, 342, n. 3 sees the solution in the unity of deed and word.

as follows: if men look only to the σάρξ of Jesus, his Incarnation as it is proclaimed and offered to them for their salvation in the Eucharist, then οὐκ ὠφελεῖ οὐδέν. Only when the words of Jesus, in which the πνεῦμα is at work, make them see the δόξα of the father in this σάρξ, only then ζωοποιεῖ (cf. xiii. 10; xv. 3). This is true for the aggravation of the σκάνδαλον in the ἀναβαίνειν of Jesus on the cross, as much as for every Eucharist, in which men naturally react just like Peter in xiii. 6. It is certainly not meant by this that one must not stop at the outward element, but must conceive of it "spiritually"— this could be suspected of being a deliberate evasion of the σκάνδαλον; but equally certainly it is not meant that one should find Life *in* the element. The point is more that in face of the scandalously visible flesh it is only in the 'strength of the Spirit that we can discern the δόξα and therefore the ζωή. This emphasis on the Word, and this demand for faith in response to it, shows that any connection between ζωή and the (sacramental) substance is even more consistently repudiated in John than it is in Paul.

The meaning of the sacraments in John has been seen[1] in the unity of spirit and matter. Just as water is first concentrated in a canal and then irrigates the country in a network of channels, so the Spirit which is principally concentrated in Jesus runs over into the sacraments; the fruits of Jesus' death are the elements, water and blood, which survive from the substance of his life and have the ability to be united with the Spirit (xix. 34–5). But this view collapses on the objections that in John σάρξ certainly does not mean matter; that the Eucharist is here understood as an aggravation of the σκάνδαλον, that is, as a challenge to faith; that in vi. 63; xv. 3 ζωή is derived from the Word alone (cf. v. 24; vi. 68; viii. 51; xii. 47); that in iii. 6–8 ὕδωρ is not referred to; and that in iv. 23–4; xx. 22–3 (otherwise than in Matt. xxviii. 19) the sacrament is not mentioned at all. In other words, the sacrament may keep its value for John, but it is certainly not central.[2]

---

[1] E.g. by Cullmann, *Early Christian Worship*, passim.

[2] Cf. Howard, *op. cit.* 147; Bultmann, *T.N.T.* II, 58. Barrett, *St. John*, 75, stresses that the sacrament does not transmit the Spirit, but the Spirit is the power which gives blessings.

The same point comes out of vii. 38–9,[1] where, as far as substance goes (there is nothing about sacrament), all that is said is that the Spirit, as the Church's life-giving water, will pour forth in the subsequent preaching by word and deed. But what is new here is the statement that the Spirit will only come after Jesus' death. This certainly corresponds to the historical facts, but takes on a special meaning for John, as the Paraclete-sayings will show.[2]

In John's account of the bestowal of the Spirit (xx. 22),[3] the Eleven are the representatives of believers in general.[4] It is possible to take this scene as a flimsy fulfilment of the Paraclete-sayings, or as a device to make good the necessary absence of Pentecost in the gospel. But this is a misunderstanding. For John, Life ($\zeta\omega\acute{\eta}$) consists in the knowledge of the true God ($\dot{a}\lambda\eta\theta\iota\nu\grave{o}\varsigma$ $\theta\epsilon\acute{o}\varsigma$) in Jesus, and the Spirit ($\pi\nu\epsilon\hat{v}\mu a$) is none other than the power of evangelism which leads to this knowledge. Hence the authority of the preaching is all important.

4. The Paraclete

It is no accident that the Paraclete is called the Spirit of truth, $\pi\nu\epsilon\hat{v}\mu a$ $\tau\hat{\eta}\varsigma$ $\dot{a}\lambda\eta\theta\epsilon\acute{\iota}a\varsigma$ (xiv. 17; xv. 26; xvi. 13), for he seems to represent reality as opposed to every kind of appearance.[5] The divine world is present in him,

[1] If these verses originally belonged together. Some (e.g. J. M. Thompson, Exp. VIII, 14 (1917), 221–2), believe 39 is a gloss.

[2] The idea in Acts ii. 33 (derived from Rabbinic theory?) may have been the origin of this statement (Knox, Acts, 85–6), but is no longer of any importance for John.

[3] Barrett, St. John, ad loc., points out the reminiscence of Gen. ii. 7; Ezek. xxxvii. 9; Wisdom xv. 11: it is life-giving new creation. On the peculiarity of this passage compared with the usual Johannine attitude, cf. Dodd, Fourth Gospel, 430.

[4] Cf. vi. 63; vii. 38. If they are to be regarded only as holders of an office (J. H. Bernard, St. John (I.C.C.), 672, 676; cf. 575 on xvii. 18; L. S. Thornton, in The Apostolic Ministry, ed. K. E. Kirk, 108–9) then the same must go for the whole of the farewell discourses, including the command to love one another. The correct view: R. N. Flew, Jesus and His Church[2], 173–4.

[5] Just as $\ddot{a}\rho\tau o\varsigma$ $\tau\hat{\eta}\varsigma$ $\zeta\omega\hat{\eta}\varsigma$, vi. 35 (cf. 33, 50–1) = that which gives $\dot{a}\lambda\acute{\eta}\theta\epsilon\iota a$ and is $\dot{a}\lambda\acute{\eta}\theta\epsilon\iota a$. On the Paraclete promises in general cf. W. M. Firor, Fulfilment of Promise, Interpretation, 7 (1953), 299–314.

just as it was present in Jesus, and will now continue to be present in his Word (xvii. 13–17).[1] It is said of him, just as of Jesus (xiv. 20), that he is in the disciples; but it is the disciples, not the world, who know him (xiv. 17) as they know Jesus (xvi. 3). Both are sent by the Father (xiv. 24, 26) and proceed from him (xvi. 27; xv. 26); both teach (vii. 14; xiv. 26), bear witness (viii. 14; xv. 26) convict the world of sin (iii. 18–20; xvi. 8–11), and at the same time do not speak on their own authority (xiv. 10; xvi. 13).[2] Thus he is only the "other Paraclete" after Jesus (xiv. 16); indeed one might be tempted to say, that there is really no place in John for the Spirit.[3] In the Paraclete Jesus comes himself (xiv. 18); and yet the Paraclete is not simply identical with Jesus; he only comes after Jesus has gone (vii. 39; xvi. 7) and whereas Jesus was only with his own for a time and will one day be with them again (xiii. 33; xiv. 3; xvi. 4; xvii. 24), the Paraclete will always be with them (xiv. 16). Jesus can be seen and yet not seen, heard and yet not heard (vi. 36; v. 37–8), he can be excluded by unbelief. Indeed, in a sense the same is true for his own, so long as he is with them (xiv. 5–11). It is only the Spirit, coming to the Church in the Word, which "brings to life"; the historical Jesus as such is the "flesh", which "profiteth nothing" (vi. 63, see above, p. 93). Only the Christ of the preaching is the Redeemer;[4] therefore it is only the Spirit of truth which really reveals Jesus to the disciples (xiv. 26; xvi. 13) and which "glorifies" him (xvi. 14). The words of the historical Jesus are almost repeated in the words of the Spirit (vi. 63; xiv. 26; xvi. 14) and this is how the historical words first gain their

[1] Howard, *op. cit.* 74.

[2] Cf. the juxtaposition of Paraclete and Jesus sayings: xiv. 15 ff. and 18 ff.; xiv. 25–6 and 21–24; xvi. 12–15 and 16–24. For the exegesis of xvi. 9, cf. Barrett, *St. John, ad loc.*

[3] E. F. Scott, q. by J. G. Simpson, *The Holy Spirit in the Fourth Gospel*, Exp. IX, 4 (1925), 293.

[4] Hence John does not make him say "I will come to you in the Spirit". Cf. Simpson, *op. cit.* 294–7. There is no theorizing here about Trinitarian inter-relationships.

power (xvi. 8–11). Hence it is here that the concept of an advocate, a helper, first makes its appearance, a concept which has wider implications than that of "revealer". Yet those very words of the Spirit are none other than those which are spoken in the authoritative preaching of the Church (xx. 22–3; xv. 26–7).[1]

Once again, therefore, it becomes apparent that John regards the Spirit as nothing other than the power of the proclamation of Jesus as Redeemer, a proclamation in which man encounters the divine world.[2] True life, ζωή, is only to be found with God, in the sphere of Spirit (this had long been the answer of a church under Hellenistic influence). God is Spirit, not flesh, and can only be approached by one who is himself in the Spirit. But what is this Spirit? In heterodox Jewish circles two quite different answers were current: (1) a heavenly substance, which is imprisoned in matter; or (2) an angel which is at work in the Good. For John, as for the whole Church, the Spirit could only be the power which makes it possible for man to recognize Jesus as the Redeemer, in whom he encounters God. In this way, in John as in Paul, the Jewish answer is given a new twist: the Spirit is the Spirit of prophecy; but this is not a phenomenon of remote ages, but is the power of God now present in the preaching of the Church, moulding the life of the Last-Age people of God and so challenging and judging the world.

E. OTHER NEW TESTAMENT WRITERS

1. *The school of Paul*

(*a*) *Ephesians*

Here the Pauline language is already somewhat diluted. The Spirit is in general the power by which the Church grows (iii. 16) and in particular the power of prayer (vi.

---

[1] Two different witnesses are not meant, naturally; it must be understood like viii. 18; III John 12 (Hoskyns, *Fourth Gospel, ad loc.*). ἔστε, instead of ἦτε, shows that the witnesses are those of all times. Cf. K. Barth, *Church Dogmatics*, E.T. IV, i. 647.
[2] Cf. Barrett, *St. John*, 76–7.

18) but, as in Paul (see above, p. 68), it is also especially the power of revelation (i. 17; iii. 5). But here we can see the influence of the primitive Christian view, in so far as the revelation concerned is thought of as a special one which is given to apostles and prophets, or can be besought for again and again by the Church, but not as the basic apprehension of the Christ-event.

> vi. 17 is a fairly traditional expression of the Spirit as working mainly through Scripture. On the other hand, in v. 18 the emphasis is rather on the ecstatic element (see above p. 65). It is probable that in iv. 4 the truth about human nature: "one body, one spirit" (ἓν σῶμα, ἓν πνεῦμα), is transferred to the Body of Christ, σῶμα Χριστοῦ, which embraces all its members within itself, so that the Spirit which works in all of them must be the one Spirit, the Spirit of the Lord (κύριος). This is surely how two further passages, ii. 18, iv. 3 are to be understood, and not in the manner of Phil. i. 27.

In other words, Ephesians comes much closer than Paul to Gnostic thought, though at the same time it approaches the views of a "pre-Gnostic" Judaism (see above pp. 15ff.). In ii. 2 the "evil spirit" makes its appearance,[1] which is at work in the damned, along with the "spiritual hosts of wickedness" (πνευματικὰ τῆς πονηρίας vi. 12) which reign in the air; moreover the typical expression, "grieving" the holy Spirit of God which is given to men, occurs in iv. 30. The Pauline conception of the Spirit as the "surety of the coming inheritance" ἀρραβὼν . . . κληρονομίας) turns up in rather sharper form in the idea of the *seal* (which is also a guarantee?) (i. 13[2] and 14; iv. 30, cf. II Cor. i. 22),[3] though there is no thought here of a substance which cannot be lost (as in James, see below p. 101).[4]

---

[1] See above, p. 24.

[2] τῆς ἐπαγγελίας stresses its eschatological bearing, as in Gal. iii. 14.

[3] Cf. Ezek. ix. 4; Lampe, *Seal of the Spirit*, 3–18.

[4] iv. 23 (ἀνανεοῦσθαι τῷ πνεύματι τοῦ νοὸς ὑμῶν), is uncertain: it is more likely to be an instrumental dative (so that νοῦς simply defines the area of the holy Spirit's activity) than dative of respect ("in your spirit" cf. Rom. xii. 2), in which case νοῦς would specify πνεῦμα as the human spirit.

(b) The Pastoral Epistles

A completely un-Pauline feature of these is the fact that Spirit only occurs six times, and one of these in the sense of "spirit of error" (I Tim. iv. 1). Out of these I Tim. iii. 16 (see above p. 57) and II Tim. iv. 22 (see above pp. 84–85)[1] are stereotyped phrases. I Tim. iv. 1 is a wholly traditional way of speaking of the prophetic Spirit. II Tim. i. 7 is close to I Cor. iv. 21. Does this mean that the Pauline conception of the Spirit as not essentially out of the ordinary has led to activities of the Spirit being replaced by Hellenistic lists of virtues? It is more probable that the day-to-day self-authentication of the Spirit had to be insisted on in the face of enthusiasts who could only see the exceptional character of their spiritual gifts. A new thought appears in Titus iii. 5 (see above p. 91 n. 4).[2] It is in good Pauline tradition that in this expression no miraculous powers are named as activities of the Spirit, but rather the new birth which admits one to justification and hope.[3] But at the same time the author himself has probably understood this as something ethical (iii. 1–3).[4]

2. Hebrews

Here the linguistic usage is complex, though strongly under Jewish influence. "Spirits" (xii. 23) are the departed (as in Judaism).[5] xii. 9 shows that behind this there is a dualistic world of flesh and spirit. This is a

---

[1] This has no reference to the grace of vocation (Dibelius, *Past.*[3], *ad loc.*).

[2] Whether πνεῦμα is taken as dependent on both phrases or only on the second makes no material difference. "The bath of a rebirth and renewal effected by the Spirit" is the most likely rendering. In any case ἀνακαινώσεως must be taken parallel with παλιγγενεσίας, not λουτροῦ.

[3] This is also a repudiation of all Hellenistic apotheosis theories (Dibelius, *ad loc.*). On the difference from Paul cf. B. S. Easton, *The Pastoral Epistles*, note *ad loc.*; E. F. Scott, *The Spirit in the N.T.*, 176–7. Another view: Flemington, *Baptism in the N.T.*, 103–4.

[4] Flemington, *op. cit.* 101.

[5] Eth. Enoch, xxii. 9; xli. 8; ciii. 3 (Wisd. iii. 1; iv. 14: ψυχαί); C. Spicq, *L'épître aux Hébreux*, II, *ad loc.*

long way from the idea that we are sons of God by virtue
of our "God-given nature". All that is said is that God
is not merely the father of mortal flesh, but also of that
innermost "I" which will one day be answerable to him.
In i. 14 angels are referred to as spirits.[1]

In iii. 7; ix. 8; x. 15 there are completely traditional
references to the Spirit speaking through scripture. In
iv. 12 "spirit" and "soul" are distinguished in purely
psychological terms, as two closely interdependent parts;
in other words the distinction is a cliché.[2] ii. 4; vi. 4–5
belong to earliest Christianity (see above, pp. 54–5) in
seeing the activity of the Spirit principally in miracles.
The first of these passages is dominated by the conception
that the Spirit of God can be divided and distributed to
individuals in different ways.[3] In the second passage the
Spirit is seen especially as a foretaste of the Age to Come.[4]
The Spirit of Grace (πνεῦμα τῆς χάριτος = Zechariah
xii. 10 LXX) in x. 29 must not be taken as a means of
salvation (despite its association with the Blood of the
Covenant); it means the Spirit as a sign of the eschatological grace of God. ix. 14 is difficult. "Christ has
offered himself unspotted to God through the everlasting
Spirit (διὰ πνεύματος αἰωνίου)". Here, too, as in xii. 9,
the contrast with flesh seems to be dominant (cf. ix. 13):
in the Old Covenant the offerings were always perishable, earthly things in the sphere of Flesh, but now
One offers himself who comes from the sphere of Spirit
and possesses the Spirit, and thus brings a redemption
which lasts far longer than the flesh.[5] "Through" (διά)
means "the ways and means" of this offering.[6]

---

[1] πνεύματα. Paul regards angels as conquered powers of the enemy:
here we are once again on orthodox Jewish ground.

[2] Spicq, op. cit. I, 52–3.

[3] πνεύματος is gen. obj., since αὐτοῦ refers to ὁ θεός (J. Moffatt, Hebrews,
I.C.C. ad loc.). The idea can be found in the O.T.

[4] The punctuation is uncertain: the easiest is to take δωρεὰ ἐπουράνιος
and πνεῦμα ἅγιον as parallel synonyms, which are then explicated in
ῥῆμα and δυνάμεις. Differently, Moffatt, ad loc.

[5] Moffatt, ad loc. compares vii. 16 and especially Midr. Ps. 31 (Str.-B.
III, 741): "formerly you were redeemed with flesh and blood . . . wherefore your redemption was temporal. But now I will redeem you by myself,
who live and remain for ever; wherefore your redemption will be eternal
redemption."

[6] Bl-Debr. §223.3. [Cf. C.F.D. Moule, Idiom-Book of N.T. Greek, 57.]

3. *The General Epistles*

(a) *James*

Apart from the purely psychological sense (ii. 26) Spirit is only spoken of in iv. 5 and there it is probably the spirit which God bestows on a man and then simply requires of him again. In point of fact, wisdom ($\sigma o\phi\acute{\iota}\alpha$) in iii. 17 is identical with this spirit.

(b) *I Peter*

Here there is a richer content. i. 11 follows tradition in limiting the prophetic Spirit to the O.T. prophets and the apostles,[1] to whom it was sent from heaven. But the difference between the time of the prophets of Scripture and the time which followed Easter is evened out: even in those days it was already the Spirit of Christ.[2] In i. 2 the Spirit is in very general terms the power of salvation.[3] iv. 14 corresponds to Jewish thought and confines the bestowal of the Spirit to the Martyrs (see above p. 27).

iii. 4: $\mathring{\eta}\sigma\acute{\nu}\chi\iota o\nu$ $\pi\nu\epsilon\hat{\nu}\mu\alpha$ has turned into a cliché.

ii. 5, see above, p. 88, n. 1.[4]

iii. 18–19 and iv. 6 present difficulties. Just as in iii. 18 (see above, p. 57) so in iv. 6 one can find two spheres mentioned, in which judgment and salvation are brought to completion, and which are certainly characterized by the substance of the body and of the Spirit which transcends the body.

There remain some questionable points.

(i) Is $\pi\nu\epsilon\acute{\nu}\mu\alpha\tau\iota$ the antecedent of $\mathring{\epsilon}\nu$ $\mathring{\hat{\omega}}$ (iii. 19)? Surely not, if this means that in the days of Noah Christ

---

[1] Overlooked by H. A. Guy, *The N.T. Doctrine of the Last Things*, 95, when he takes this here and in Acts to mean the breaking-in of the Eschaton.

[2] The B reading (omitting $X\rho\iota\sigma\tau o\hat{\nu}$) is a later attempt to remove the sting. There is something similar in Barn. v. 6; Ign. *Mag.* ix. 2; Just. *Apol.* lxii. 3–4.

[3] = II Thess. ii. 13. Corresponding to $\theta\epsilon o\hat{\nu}$ $\pi\alpha\tau\rho\acute{o}s$ and $\mathring{\prime}I\eta\sigma o\hat{\nu}$ $X\rho\iota\sigma\tau o\hat{\nu}$, $\pi\nu\epsilon\acute{\nu}\mu\alpha\tau os$ (I Pet. i. 2) can only be taken as a subjective genitive. The triadic formulation has progressed a long way; but even so the Spirit still comes before Christ. See below, p. 108, n. 3.

[4] Selwyn, *I Peter*, following E. Lohmeyer, sees the Eucharist in the "spiritual sacrifices". Cf. *contra* F. W. Beare, *I Peter*, *ad loc.* Cf. also R. N. Flew, *Jesus and His Church*, 160.

8+

was already preaching in the spirit to those who are now in prison (cf. Ign. *Mag.* ix. 2). A possible idea would be that Christ, after the crucifixion, went as a disembodied spirit to the spirits, but it is fairly certain that here, as in i. 6; iv. 4 ἐν ᾧ only means "and so".[1] In which case the Resurrection is not to be distinguished from ζωοποιηθῆναι as a second event, but rather the fact of the Resurrection is explicated in the descent into hell and the ascension into heaven. It remains to ask whether both come to the same thing, in other words whether the φυλακή is to be thought of as being "under way" in the air. If it is correct to reconstruct an old formula from this passage, then this was the original sense. In the present context the two are separated from each other.

(ii) Are the πνεύματα demons or the departed? Since iv. 6 cannot be separated from this passage, they must be the departed. However, it is possible that in a rather obscure way the demons (perhaps at work in their successors) are included too. But would they be placed in Hades?

(iii) Who are the νεκροί in iv. 6? Despite the combination of literal and spiritual meanings of "living" and "dead" in Hermas, s. IX. xvi. 3–6, it is very difficult to refer the word here to those who are still alive on earth but spiritually dead, particularly because the formula in iv. 5 can hardly be interpreted in this way. But it is also highly improbable that deceased Christians who heard the Gospel during their lives are meant.[2] Along with iii. 19, one must take them to be the πνεύματα who are named there.[3]

(iv) In which case, what is σάρξ? When iv. 6 is compared with iii. 18 and I Cor. v. 5 (see above, p. 85), it can only be a judgment in the earthly sphere, i.e. death, which is in question. κριθῶσιν (iv. 6) must therefore be understood as a pluperfect.

(c) *II Peter and Jude*

Here the Spirit is by now only the inspired power of the now canonical Scriptures (i. 21). In Jude, on the other

---

[1] [Cf. C. F. D. Moule, *Idiom-Book of N.T. Greek*, 131–2.]

[2] So Beare (*I Peter, ad loc.*) against Selwyn (*I Peter*, 338–9).

[3] The *Gospel of St. Peter*, 41, suggests the deceased.

hand, it is, in Gnostic fashion, the mark of the "un-psychic", coming out especially in prayer.[1]

(d) I John

The Spirit is understood principally in a primitive Christian way as the visible sign of the great turning-point; but the new factor which is recognized by this is no longer simply the breaking-in of the Eschaton but is the abiding of Christ in believers (iii. 24; iv. 13).[2] This explains why once again there is no emphasis on the extraordinariness of the gifts of the Spirit. It is true that the Spirit is clearly grasped as a gift from outside, which is in no sense innate (iv. 13);[3] nevertheless, as in John, the Spirit again bears witness; in one place it is said to do this com-prehensively in "water" and "blood" (v. 6) but it also, in a narrower sense, is independent of these (v. 7); that is, when it is the power of preaching, which, after the sacra-ment, is to an especial degree an activity of the Spirit.[4] The same conception of the testifying prophetic Spirit appears in iv. 1–6; but here the Johannine concept (see above p. 97) is combined with that of the two mutually hostile spirits,[5] and the result comes to precise expression in I John iv. 6. Fully Christian is the naming of the opposing force as Antichrist (iv. 3) and especially the confession of the Incarnate Lord as a criterion of manifestations of the Spirit (see above p. 65). Animistic concepts

---

[1] On 19–20 see above, p. 87. In 20–1 the πνεῦμα ἅγιον is subordinate to θεός and κύριος ἡμῶν Ἰησοῦ Χριστοῦ (see below, p. 108, n. 3).

[2] This is of course the eschatological fulfilment; but it is understood in a way very different from that of the primitive church, cf. Guy, *op. cit.* 171.

[3] The Spirit is still superior and generic (ἐκ).

[4] But here the Sacraments do not carry the Spirit, though they are important precisely because it is through them that the prophetic πνεῦμα proclaims the Life and Death of Jesus as real events. That the Baptism in Jordan was the real moment of redemption, and that the death of Jesus only had the function of making the Spirit which had been received there available to believers (Flemington, *op. cit.* 89–91), was acceptable to Gnostic opponents. But the author means more than that, as i. 7 shows.

[5] Test. Jud. xx. 1: τὸ τῆς ἀληθείας καὶ τὸ τῆς πλάνης (πνεῦμα). Cf. above, pp. 17–18.

have left a somewhat deeper impression here. Nowhere else in the New Testament is there such an emphasis on trust in the Spirit which is at work in the Church, which dispenses with all official authority, and which bears true testimony in bringing, not new, unheard-of revelations, but the old message.

4. *The Apocalypse*

That the Apocalypse occupies a place of its own in the New Testament is true also in respect to its theory of the Spirit, which has clear affinities in "pre-Gnostic" Jewish circles. Both here and in popular Judaism,[1] unclean demon-spirits appear as "spirits", πνεύματα (xvi. 13–14; xviii. 2), and the pure vital life-force as the "Spirit" given by God, or, it might be, by a demon (xi. 11; xiii. 15). But the dominant concept is that of the Spirit of Prophecy (xix. 10). This is evidently thought of as an abnormal phenomenon; the state of "being in the Spirit" is distinguished from an habitual state (i. 10; iv. 2). The Spirit is the power which bestows a countenance which a man does not normally have. It can "lead him away" (xvii. 3; xxi. 10) into miraculous places which the natural man does not see.[2] Therefore in xi. 8 "spiritually" (πνευματικῶς) means in prophetic, as opposed to normal, language.[3] But this Spirit has not merely been at work in the past. It speaks to-day. Its task is not just to recall the promises of scripture; it gives them

[1] See Eth. Enoch, *passim*; E. F. Scott, *The Spirit in the N.T.* 212. Without the Apocalypse we would not know how primitive the conceptions of the Spirit were in the Christian community. But is the lack of a *doctrine* of the Spirit not due to the fact that here, as throughout primitive Christianity, all the stress is laid on the future, not on the presence of the Spirit?

[2] Yet cf. ἐν (contrasted with Mark i. 12, where the reality of the change of place is unambiguously stressed).

[3] The interpretation "allegorically" is impossible. A text referring to Sodom or Egypt is not transferred to Jerusalem, nor is Jerusalem given an allegorical disguise. No, Jerusalem is seen with prophetic eyes and identified with the Biblical Sodom and Egypt.

new expression (xiv. 13). Consequently its superhuman divinity is felt so strongly that the human speaker can drop out altogether.[1] In the Apocalypse, the Spirit always speaks to the Church, and the person through whom it speaks is of secondary importance. To this extent, the Spirit is associated with the Church and not with the individual.[2] But the Spirit—and this is decisive—is none other than the Ascended Lord himself (ii. 1 = 7, 8 = 11 etc.), even if it is the Ascended Lord in his function of speaking to the Church : for only as the Spirit is he with his own. (Such a thing is never said of the Lord ($\kappa\acute{u}\rho\iota\sigma$) himself;[3] he is entirely in heaven.) That is why in xxii. 17 it can be said that the Spirit and the Bride say "Come". When the Church, in the power of the Spirit,[4] calls for her Lord, it is ultimately not her own power and piety, but the Lord himself, who calls. Yet at the same time the Spirit, as the power proceeding from the Lord, can be distinguished from the Lord himself (see above p. 60).

This tension comes clearly to light once again in the strange notion of the seven spirits. From the point of view of the history of religion, they are simply the seven archangels.[5] In the Apocalypse, they stand between God and Christ, and Grace and Peace proceed from them (i. 4);[6] they stand like lamps before God's throne, as the angels do (iv. 5);[7] they are sent out over the whole earth as messengers of God and Christ (v. 6); together with the angels of the churches (i. 20), they are in the hand of

---

[1] ii. 7; xiv. 13; xxii. 17.

[2] Lohmeyer, *Apok.* on ii. 28.

[3] *Idem ibid.* 186; cf. the Johannine Paraclete.

[4] On the parataxis cf. Acts v. 32; John xv. 26–7.

[5] Tobit xii. 15. Another view: G. H. Dix, *The Seven Archangels and the Seven Spirits*, J.T.S. 28 (1927), 233–50, who suggests the influence of the 7-branched candlestick (iv. 5). For the number seven cf. Zech. iv. 2, 10 (Rev. v. 6); Philo, *Op. Mund.* 99–128.

[6] The passage is certainly not interpolated (*contra* Lohmeyer, *Apok.*; R. H. Charles, *Revelation*, I.C.C. *ad loc.*).

[7] viii. 2; cf. Syr. Baruch. xxi. 6; Ps.–Clem. *Hom.* viii. 13. Differently Str.-B. III, 788.

Christ (iii. 1). Thus they represent the Spirit of God in its fullness and completeness,[1] while at the same time they represent the angels of the throne and correspond to the angels of the churches.

This can only be understood against the background of "pre-Gnostic" Jewish thought. Exactly the same concept, perfected by Gnosticism, can be found in Valentine. There the angels are simply Christ himself, but now it is the individualized Christ, the Christ who comes to the individual, and who is at the same time the alter-ego of the human spirit ($\pi\nu\epsilon\hat{\upsilon}\mu\alpha$).[2] The only essential difference is that the Apocalypse is a Church book and ascribes the Spirit, not to the individual, but to the Church.[3] By now, the process was already complete by which the Spirit of God had become that individual spirit which is given to each man as "his" spirit, and similarly the identity of this spirit (which proceeds from God) with the newly-given "self" of a man was well established. But since the thought of the Apocalypse begins with the Church and not with the individual, the "seven churches" correspond with the "seven spirits" which are just as much the "new, grace-endowed self" of the Church, as they are the works of the Spirit, proceeding from God, with which the Church is endowed; and in their totality they are nothing other than the one Spirit of God.

That the Spirits are thought of as angels no longer presents any difficulties. The two are frequently interchanged.[4] It is already the case in heterodox Judaism that the figures of angels have almost the same rank as God or as the Messiah.[5] The angel appears as a mediator

[1] As *Spiritus Septiformis*, Isa. xi. 2. The Hebrew text knows only six gifts of the Spirit, LXX and Syrian versions arrive one way or another at seven. Cf. Charles, *Revelation*, on i. 4.

[2] See above, p. 21. Cf. G. Quispel in Eranos Jbch. 15 (1947), 264: "L'ange est le Christ rapporté à l'existence individuelle de l'homme spirituel". Cf. also Cl. Al. *Exc. Theod.* xii. 2 (angels = $\pi\nu\epsilon\acute{\upsilon}\mu\alpha\tau\alpha$ $\nu o\epsilon\rho\acute{\alpha}$).

[3] Loh. *Ap.* on ii. 28.

[4] See above, p. 17, n. 1; also Herm. m. XI, 9; Rev. xvii. 3; xxi. 10.

[5] IV Ezra v. 43; Eth. Enoch xxxix. 5–7.

between God and man, who intercedes for men and brings
their prayers before God.[1]   That is why the triad, God-
Christ-angels, is so common, even in the Apocalypse.[2]
Just as it is true throughout the Apocalypse that God's
activity is represented in concrete, personal forms, and
yet remains his own activity, this is true also of the
seven angel-spirits, who are simply the personal activity
of God.[3]

[1] Test. L. v. 6–7; D. vi. 2; cf. R. H. Charles, *Apocrypha and Pseudepigrapha*, II, 307, 335; Tobit xii. 15
[2] Luke ix. 26; I Tim. v. 21; Rev. iii. 5.
[3] Cf. also M. Kiddle, *Revelation* (Moffatt N.T. Commentary) on
Rev. iv. 6.

APPENDIX: THE APOSTOLIC FATHERS

In the period that immediately follows, the development can be followed under three heads.

(i) The Gnostic-substantial tradition (see above, pp. 20–23). That Christ is composed of a spiritual substance becomes more and more important. It is true even of the Pre-existent One (see above, p. 61 and II Clement ix. 5; xiv. 2, Hermas s. IX, i. 1). Ignatius, although he maintains the Jewish doctrine of resurrection in opposition to Gnosis, nevertheless reveals a tendency to think along Gnostic lines: the union of spirit and flesh-substance in Christ makes possible the resurrection of the flesh of the believer (*Eph.* vii. 2; *Mag.* i. 2; *Sm.* iii. 2–3; xii. 2).

(ii) The ecstatic tradition. The Spirit is replaced by extraordinary psychical phenomena (see above, p. 65 n. 6).[1] In due course it comes to be thought that these are a kind of reward for exceptional faith (cf. I Clem. ii. 2).

(iii) The official Church tradition. It is no longer so, that a man whom God marks out by the gift of the Spirit is appointed to a particular ministry, but rather the man who is duly appointed to an office is guaranteed to possess the Spirit of God along with it. II Tim. i. 16 is corroborated by I Tim. iv. 14; i. 18. Ign. *Phld.* vii. 1–2; *Mag.* xiii. 1; I Clem. xli–xlii (but. cf. xlii. 4) are more doubtful. Irenaeus is the first to put it unequivocally: *qui cum episcopatus successione charisma veritatis certum . . . acceperunt* (*Haer.* IV, xxvi. 2).[2] Nevertheless the Kerygma of the New Testament preserves its power, and in the succeeding centuries it will again and again make new conquests.[3]

[1] Herm. v. I, i. 3; II, i. 1.

[2] Cf. W. D. Davies, *Light on the Ministry from the N.T.*, Religion in Life, 21 (1952), 267–8.

[3] On the question of Trinitarian formulae see further Ign. *Mag.* xiii. 1–2. In the repeated ἐν (xiii. 1) and in the expressions in I Clem. xlvi. 6; lviii. 2. there is discernible a slight hesitation in making the Spirit fully equal to God and Christ.

INDEX OF REFERENCES

8*